Pub Lover's Guide to Ontario

By Bill Perrie

Warwick Publishing
Toronto

This book is dedicated to my wife Debbie, for having belief and supplying me with "lunch" money (400 pubs in four months — 'nuff said).

Visit our web site: www.publovers.com

Pub Lover's Guide to Ontario
© 2002 by Bill Perrie

We acknowledge the financial support of the Government of Canada through the Book Publishing Industry Development Program for our publishing activities.

ISBN: 1-894622-23-5

Published by Warwick Publishing Inc.
161 Frederick Street
Toronto, Ontario M5A 4P3 Canada
www.warwickgp.com

Distributed in Canada by:
General Distribution Services Ltd.
325 Humber College Blvd.
Toronto, ON M9W 7C3

Distributed in the United States by:
LPC Group
22 Broad Street, Milford, CT 06460 USA

Printed and bound in Canada

Enjoy at your favourite local pub.

Davis Skill Games

Pub Locations

GUINNESS. PURE GENIUS.

Acknowledgements

To John Morrison for all the help with the photographs, to Jim at Warwick Publishing for having faith, and to the many people I met on the way — the owners who talked of their pubs with pride, the bartenders who filled me in on the daily events and pulled a great pint, and finally fellow pub lovers who shared a drink and then pointed me in the right direction — I thank you all.

If you have a favourite pub that you would like to see in the *Pub Lover's Guide*, please drop me a line at

publovers@rogers.com

Introduction

THE ONTARIO VERSION of the British- and Irish-style pub has come a long way. A decade ago they were few and far between and mostly patronized by people like myself trying to recapture a former "Old Country" existence. Now they are a growing and vibrant part of neighbourhoods from Windsor to Ottawa.

The greatest change is that young people are preferring the atmosphere and comfort of the "local" pub; they are well educated in the brand choices on offer and can be seen drinking beers that were perhaps the choices of their grandfathers. The industry has been quick to notice this and many pubs have added big-screen TVs, video games and additions to their traditional menus to capture a piece of this vast market.

The number of pubs in Ontario has almost doubled in the last five years, while other establishments, such as the sports bar, have slowly declined. I took it upon myself (as a good citizen) to take four months off work and find the best of them. Unable to obtain client lists from the breweries, I decided to ask the experts — pub lovers — where their favourite places were in Ontario. Armed with a few dozen names, my journey had begun. As more people heard of my quest, more e-mails started to come in, some from towns I had never heard of and many from places that to me had been just exit signs on the highway.

The first thing to hit me was that, while many of the new pubs were catering to the modern age, there were also many still basking in the light of yesteryear. Many, such as the Copper Kettle in Glen Williams, were a trip down memory lane to the days of sawdust on the floors, a piano in the corner and good pub grub homemade on the premises. Or the Old Mill in Ashton, with its Tudor-style exterior looking like a Constable painting as it sits on the banks of the Jock River. Then there were the Victorian homes where the publicans have preserved the grandeur of the old manse and maintained the old gardens, such as Dr. Dillane's in

Schomberg and the Prince Albert in Mount Albert. The list goes on, to modern pubs like Windy O'Neills in Vaughan, which has gone to great lengths to duplicate a turn-of-the-century authentic Dublin pub (and has succeeded).

The bottom line is, there is so much diversity in the Ontario pub scene that there is something for everyone. From those who prefer the serenity of a small country pub, to the live music fan, to the sports fan — all these people enjoy the good food, the courteous staff and the friendship found in their favourite "local." The Ontario pub, my friends, is alive and well and coming to a neighbourhood near you.

❖

THE CROW'S NEST PUB

Newmarket's Best Kept Secret

the British Isles Show

British Isles Show 2002

March 1st, 2nd, 3rd.

Queen Elizabeth Building
National Trade Centre
Toronto
For Further Information
Call: 905-454-0607

or Email: bmartinpromotions@on.aibn.com

BRITAIN

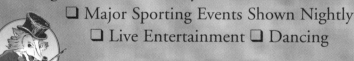

Pub Listings

The Winchester Arms

Address: 59 Victoria Street West, Alliston
Telephone: 705-435-6358
Proprietors: Mike and Tammy
Opened: 1996
Bar: 13 Draft Taps

The richly carpeted main bar area has long, green velvet bench seating; an adjoining elevated dining section is sectioned off by open bookshelves and contains green leather high-backed booths. The elegant Dominion Room with capacity for 30 people is available for small parties and meetings. A pool table sits in another section opposite the bar. The bar has a separate area known as Piccadilly Circus where children under 12 can play in a supervised environment while their parents enjoy a moment's peace having dinner next door. For a minimal fee the children can eat and play; please call the bar for playroom times. The menu is varied with the following specials: Monday — Fish and chips; Tuesday — Kids eat free; Wednesday — Wings; Friday and Saturday — Chef's special, and Sunday features a roast of the day dinner special. Trivia contests are held twice monthly for prizes and entertainment is offered periodically; please call for details on both.

Ajax

Magwyers Pub

Address: 105 Bayly Street West, Ajax
Telephone: 905-426-8877
Proprietor: Norman Shunda
Opened: 1998
Bar: 24 Draft Taps

Situated in the middle of a busy plaza, this small pub takes full advantage of the heavy pedestrian traffic by offering quality economical lunch specials. The sit-down bar, which is a step up to the right, is busy with after-work regulars. A selection of single malts is available. The menu is a mix of traditional/North American fare with a good selection of steak dinners. Evening specials are as follows: Sunday — Traditional roast beef dinner; Monday — Mussel madness; Tuesday — Wings, Wednesday; Ribs; Thursday — T-bone steaks; Friday — Fish; and Saturday — Prime rib. An oyster bar is featured regularly throughout the year; please call for details.

❖

The Portly Piper

Address: 235 Bayly Street West, Ajax
Telephone: 905-426-9535
Proprietor: Dan Ranch
Opened: 2001
Bar: 22 Draft Taps

The sit-down bar area is a few steps up from the main level with plenty of seating and perimeter tables. The dining room has comfortable booths along with a central gas fireplace and large-screen TV. A room off to the side contains a pool table and golf game, the bar also has an area set aside for darts. The bar runs a promotion with a nearby comedy club whereby they sell you two tickets for the price of one and the club in return will issue a voucher for free appetizers back at the pub. The menu has many traditional dishes and a section called the Butcher's Block which offers exceptional marinated steak kabobs. Entertainment every Friday and Saturday evening and the occasional Thursday features 3 M.D.M.

Raven and Firkin

Address: 67 Kingston Road East, Ajax
Telephone: 905-426-5110
Proprietor: Gavin Neumann
Opened: 2000
Bar: 16 Draft Taps

When you enter the front doors of this English-style pub the bar is immediately in front of you and there are dining sections to either side; the elevated non-smoking section is to the right and furnished with a mixture of booths and tables. To the rear of the Raven you will find the pool tables and Golden Tee golf games. There are 12 TVs throughout the bar for all major sporting events. With a full menu containing traditional fare and more, the pub has a choice of eight food specials daily. The wings are on special Monday, Wednesday and Thursday evenings. Entertainment features a disc jockey every Thursday night and periodical throughout the month; please call for details.

The Thirsty Monk

Address: 85 Kingston Road East, Ajax
Telephone: 905-427-5859
Proprietors: Christien, Antoine and Julian
Opened: 2000
Bar: 22 Draft Taps

An open concept and high ceilings gives an almost amphitheatre effect to this popular Ajax pub. The sit-down bar is a few steps down from the main level and has two large semi-circular booths opposite. Among the many draft beers you will find three house brands, namely Monk red, lager and light. A separate room seating 20 on the upper level can be reserved for office parties, group lunches or dinners, etc. The pub also has table top football as well as a pool table and, out back, a large patio that seats approximately one hundred. The extensive menu includes home-made pastas, seafood and traditional pub fare. All major soccer games on two large screens. A DJ plays Thursday nights and live bands on the Saturday.

❖

The Wallace Arms
Address: 967 Westney Road South, Ajax
Telephone: 905-428-8790
Proprietors: The Wallace family
Opened: 1997
Bar: 11 Draft Taps

This pub is focussed on creating a meeting place where people can come to talk and, in the words of the owners, "where neighbours become friends." A large portion of the clientele are from the old country and many state that this pub more than any other reminds them of the pubs back there. The Wallace family are all from Glasgow and add to the authenticity of the place. A large mixed menu with many traditional favourites is offered. Monday and Tuesday are wing nights and are claimed to be the best in the area, with many customers travelling a good distance for them. Saturdays and Sundays see a breakfast menu which includes a large Scottish/Irish breakfast plate. Entertainment on Friday and Saturday nights.

Aurora

Filly and Firkin
Address: 14888 Yonge Street, Aurora
Telephone: 905-727-4271
Manager: Angela MacNeill
Opened: 1992
Bar: 16 Draft Taps

As you enter the front door the sit-down bar area is to the right and a dartboard section to the left, the pub then opens up to a dining area containing two side-by side sections of booths. The back leads out to a charming courtyard patio. The menu is varied and features an excellent selection of daily specials. Monday the pub offers half-price mussels with your choice of sauce and a fresh French stick; Tuesday has half-price Firkin famous beef ribs, and Wednesdays are wing nights. Thursday entertainment features live bands and Friday is a disc jockey and Anaconda trivia with prizes. A Sunday tradition in Aurora is the long-running karaoke show with cash prizes.

❖

The Old Mill
Address: 113 Old Mill Road, Ashton
Telephone: 613-257-4423
Proprietor: Val Broeders
Opened: 1986
Bar: 11 Draft Taps

The picturesque village of Ashton lies on the border of Ottawa and Lancashire counties and is a short drive south from Highway 7. This beautiful pub is situated in an old grist mill with a Tudor exterior. Inside, there is a small sit-down bar at one end and a large stone fireplace in the dining area. The walls have different themes, including one featuring the works of local artists; another depicts regulars at their "best" and is cheekily called "The Wall of Shame." An old piano sits in the bar and has been used for many an impromptu party. The backyard patio has a wonderful view overlooking the Jock river and woodlands. The menu is mainly traditional with most dishes baked on the premises; a vegetarian daily special and a kids' menu are also available. Saturday night features a jazz band, while Sunday afternoon is open mike from 2 PM. until 6 PM.

The Badger's Rest
Address: 15570 Yonge Street, Aurora
Telephone: 905-841-3332
Proprietor: Sue Naylor
Opened: 2001
Bar: 15 Draft Taps

This English-style pub has an open concept with an upper dining section. The pub area has comfortable bench seating and an L-shaped sit-down bar. A CD featuring the best local bands was recorded here to raise funds for charity. The menu is extensive and features many favourites, with the fish and chips being by far the most popular. Evening specials as follows: Monday — Wings and draft; Tuesday — Two-for-one T-bone steaks; Wednesday — Ladies' night featuring half-price appetizers; Friday — Free roast beef at the bar from 4 PM to 6 PM and Sundays the popular two-for-one fish and chips. Thursday night is retro 80s with disc jockey, and Fridays and Saturdays feature the best in live entertainment. The bar also boasts the best darts team in Aurora.

Jersey Joe's

Address: 14987 Yonge Street, Aurora
Telephone: 905-727-4181
Proprietors: The Badali Family
Opened: 1988
Bar: 11 Draft Taps

The elevated bar area contains a small sit-down bar with a small section of two tables, here you will find regulars who have come to be more like family, many of them enjoying the hospitality of this friendly pub from day one. The main dining area has four large booths down one wall while the opposite wall has a central brick fireplace. There's a large pull-down screen for all major soccer games and other sporting events. The menu has a good cross-section of traditional and North American pub fare. Tuesday is wing day, Wednesday is half-price pizza and Friday is a marvelous prime rib dinner. Entertainment every Friday featuring the king of karaoke, Laser Larry.

Barrie

The Beefeater Arms

Address: 29 Dunlop Street, Barrie
Telephone: 705-722-7227
Proprietors: Tony and Gail Caven
Opened: 2000
Bar: 14 Draft Taps

In the heart of Barrie's downtown, the Beefeater is a very traditional English-style pub. The downstairs is long and narrow with the sit-down bar to your left and the main dining area towards the far end. Upstairs has dartboards, shuffleboard and a pool table; this area with a full-service bar can also be booked for private functions and events. The pub is also a main sponsor and home to the Barrie rugby club. Twice a year the busy street is closed for festivities and the pub puts a patio out front. The menu is traditional pub fare with many daily specials. Live entertainment Saturday nights.

The Bull and Barrel

Address: 75 Cedar Pointe Drive, Unit 901, Barrie
Telephone: 705-726-5757
Proprietors: Rick and Carol
Opened: 1996
Bar: 12 Draft Taps

This friendly local pub has traditional décor and a cozy fireplace along with a small sit-down bar where you will find it hard not to join in the conversation with the regulars. Rick and Carol pride themselves on the high quality of their food, much of which is homemade and prepared fresh on the premises. The menu has a great selection ranging from traditional sandwiches to steaks and pizzas. The pizzas are deliciously different and depending on your background you can have it Irish, Scottish or English. Wings are on special every night. Entertainment every Saturday, with Celtic music featured on the last Saturday of the month.

Wickie's

Address: 274 Burton Avenue, Barrie
Telephone: 705-725-0630
Proprietors: Renee` and Chris
Opened: 1988
Bar: 15 Draft Taps

A light interior and many windows give this pub a very bright, spacious look. A favourite hang-out of soccer fans for many years, Wickie's shows all major soccer games from England and Scotland on a large screen. A games room at the back features four pool tables and dartboards. As well as soccer games, this pub shows all major sports including Nascar. The first million-dollar N.T.N. trivia game prize was won in Wickie`s. The menu is traditional pub fare and more, with wings on special every day. A large outdoor patio is screened from the nearby traffic by wood partitions.

The Fox and Fiddle

Address: 407 Bayfield Street, Barrie
Telephone: 705-726-9996
General Managers: Jerry and Danielle
Opened: 1999
Bar: 24 Draft Taps

A square cherry-oak sit-down bar sits in the centre of this large pub/restaurant, giving it an almost *Cheers-* like feel. The dining area has plenty of booths with traditional burgundy upholstery. A large fireplace separates this area from the tables of the non -smoking section. A large open patio has a garden look, with many plants and flowering hanging baskets. The menu is a mix of traditional and North American fare, with many daily specials.

Monday and Tuesday are wing nights. The most popular food special is on Thursday nights when it's all-you-can-eat pasta; the line-ups start early and are soon out the door. The chefs cook the pasta made to order in full view and then deliver the meal to the tables personally. Entertainment every Friday and Saturday nights.

Bayfield

The Albion Hotel

Address: 1 Main Street, Bayfield
Telephone: 519-565-2641
Proprietor: Kim
Opened: 1857
Bar: 12 Draft Taps

This historical hotel was built in 1840 as a store. An addition was added in 1857, and it has opened its doors as a hotel ever since. One of the oldest licensed establishments in Canada, the management and staff of the Albion are very proud of its heritage. The hotel features a casual dining room, a cozy pub and four bed and breakfast rooms. The menu has Texmex, pizzas and a large selection of main entrees, including traditional fare and succulent steaks. The staff are only too pleased to tell customers the history of this grand old lady. Entertainment periodical; please call for details.

Belleville

The Red Lion

Address: 211 Coleman Street, Belleville
Telephone: 613-966-2458
Proprietors: The Mofina family
Opened: 1995
Bar: 12 Draft Taps

The bar sits on the bank of the Moira river and many of the tables are by windows overlooking it as it flows on to Lake Ontario. The bar has dartboards and a pool table and at one end an old piano that customers are welcome to play. The pub is nicknamed "The Dawghouse," as it is a main sponsor and home to the Belleville Bulls rugby club. The menu is mostly pub fare, with the claim of having the best burgers in town. Entertainment every Friday night.

The Winchester Arms
Address: 173 Dundas Street East, Belleville
Telephone: 613-966-7060
Proprietor: John Lee
Opened: 1997
Bar: 13 Draft Taps

The large central sit-down bar stretches from the flagstone-floored pub to the richly carpeted dining room in this striking Tudor building. Booths line the perimeter of the pub and many are flanked by stain glass windows. A separate banquet room with a capacity of 50 is available for private functions. The menu is very varied and includes traditional pub fare. Evening specials are as follows: Monday — Fish and Chips; Tuesday — Curry night; Wednesday — Wings; Thursday — Prime rib; Friday — Chef's Special; Saturday: Steak Night, and Sunday is a three-course special. Entertainment twice monthly, please call for details.

Bolton

The Toby Jug
Address: 15 Allen Drive, Bolton
Telephone: 905-857-7494/Web: http://www.tobyjug.ca
Proprietors: Ron, Tom and the two Helens
Opened: 1989
Bar: 11 Draft Taps

With the owners hailing from Scotland there is more than a little Scottish flair to this friendly neighbourhood pub. A large stone fireplace takes pride of place in the centre of the room and the walls are decorated with many Scottish pictures and posters. A loyal clientele are always ready for some friendly banter at the bar where the common topic is the plight of their football teams back in Britain. The pub shows most major soccer games. Three large mirrors shipped over from Liverpool line the wall behind the bar and the shelves are full of toby jugs that have been collected over the years. The menu is very traditional with a good selection of steak pies.

The Braemar

Address: 7 Division Street, Bowmanville
Telephone: 905-623-4579
Proprietors: Jimmy and Elizabeth
Opened: 2000
Bar: 19 Draft Taps

A touch of Scotland in Bowmanville, this pub has lots of Scottish memorabilia on all walls and is proud to promote its heritage. A separate dining room to one side and a large backroom which can be booked for functions is lined with many dartboards. No jugs of beer here but they do sell at a special price a 40-oz. pint. The patio sits around a majestic oak that provides a welcome natural shade on sunnier days. The menu is traditional Scottish fare and even includes haggis and neep. A great collection of over 50 single malts is available. Entertainment every Thursday by the well-known Johnny Blue, live music every Friday and Saturdays periodical.

The Winchester Arms

Address: 109 King Street, Bowmanville
Telephone: 905-623-6744
General Manager: Lisa
Opened: 1997
Bar: 13 Draft Taps

The bookcase partition as seen in a few of the Winchesters is an attractive feature of the bar and adds a touch of privacy to the dining area. The outside of the building is Tudor-style and the rear of the pub looks out onto a green belt. A small dart room is great for the novice who wants to practice unseen. Menu is a traditional/Canadian mix with the following evening specials: Monday — Fish and chips; Tuesday — Two-for-one pasta; Wednesday — Wings; Thursday — Buy one meal, get one free; Friday — ask server for details; Saturday: Steak night, and Sunday is a roast beef dinner. Complimentary munchies at the bar every Friday from 4 PM to 6 PM. Every evening from 9 PM until close wings are on special.

The Winchester Arms
Address: 4 Holland Street West, Bradford
Telephone: 905-775-0145
General Manager: Claire Debney
Opened: 1994
Bar: 13 Draft Taps

Located on Bradford's busy four corners, this Winchester is a popular lunchtime spot. English-style décor with comfortable bench seating in the bar area and an adjoining games room with pool table and dartboards; this room can also be booked for private functions. The menu is a traditional–Canadian mix with the following evening specials: Monday — Fish and chips; Tuesday — Family night (kids eat free); Wednesday — Wings; Thursday — Pasta and ribs alternate; Friday and Saturday: Chef's special; Sunday: traditional roast (varies weekly). Wings are also on special 4 PM to 6 PM daily and after 11 PM on Friday, Saturday and Sundays. Entertainment periodical, please call for details.

Brampton

The Clock and Hen
Address: 71 West Drive, Unit 35, Brampton
Telephone: 905-456-1051
Proprietor: Brian Martin
Opened: 1996
Bar: 18 Draft Taps

A popular Irish-style bar, with many of the regulars hailing from the Emerald Isle. Owner Brian Martin is also the organizer of the annual British Isles show and it is not unusual to see a member of the *Coronation Street* cast back at the bar after the show; indeed, one year "Curly Watts" got up and jammed on the stage. This pub is also a great Terry Fox Run fundraiser and on that day the car park is taken over by live bands and the party goes all day until close. The menu is varied, with many Irish traditional dishes, a big favourite being the steak-and-Guinness pie. A big screen features all major soccer games. Live entertainment every Friday and Saturday night.

❖

The Crown and Anchor

Address: 305 Charolais Boulevard, Brampton
Telephone: 905-453-5270
Proprietor: Karmjit Upaul
Opened: 1993
Bar: 13 Draft Taps

Situated in a small plaza, the bar is to the right as you walk in the pub and the dining area to the left. At the back of the bar are dartboards and a pool table. A small courtyard patio is fenced off from the parking lot adding privacy to summer-time meals. The menu is a traditional/Canadian mix and Friday nights are very busy for the prime rib dinner special. Once a month the pub hosts an international food theme night; previous nights have been Mexican and Arabian. Entertainment every Friday and Saturday night.

The Crown and Anchor

Address: 14 Lisa Street, Brampton
Telephone: 905-451-4811
Proprietors: The Bowie family
Opened: 1996
Bar: 9 Draft Taps

This small traditional British pub was taken over by the Bowie family in 1996 and since then they have created an authentic cozy pub atmosphere. Many of the regulars are from the British Isles and Friday afternoons at the bar are always a good laugh with the dry British humour in abundance. The menu is traditional, and a pub favourite is the fish and chips, which because of the batter many say are the best in town. All major soccer games shown; entertainment is monthly so please call for details.

❖

Donnelly's

Address: 237 Queen Street East, Brampton
Telephone: 905-451-7137
Proprietor: Tony Donnelly
Opened: 1994
Bar: 12 Draft Taps

A large open-concept pub, Donnelly's is one the best-known bars in the Greater Toronto Area for many reasons, one being its role as a gathering place for Scottish fans whenever the national team is on duty, and where else can you get John Blue entertaining two nights in a row? The bar has two pool tables and a juke box. The menu is traditional pub fare with homemade steak pies which, according to regulars, are the best in Brampton. Plenty of daily specials, most of which are made fresh on the premises. Live bands on Thursdays and Sundays, and John Blue Friday and Saturday nights.

Frigate and Firkin

Address: 378 Queen Street East, Brampton
Telephone: 905-456-8060
Proprietor: Diego Gulino
Opened: 19
Bar: 16 Draft Taps

Located just off the 410 on busy Queen Street, the Frigate is the perfect stop after a busy commute. The long sit-down bar is to the right as you go in and the pub features many booths and tables. The newly expanded patio is a very popular summer evening spot. Billed as the "Un*Frigate*able" pub, the menu features a large mix of traditional grub, ribs, steaks and seafood. A weekend brunch is also available, along with many daily and weekly specials. The bar has two pool tables and features free pool from 3 to 6 PM Monday to Friday. Four dartboards, mega touch games and the golden tee golf game round out the recreational choices. The Frigate also shows all major live boxing events on its big screens.

The Ivy Bridge

Address: 160 Main Street South, Brampton
Telephone: 905-453-2337
Proprietor: Bill O`Beirne
Opened: 1993
Bar: 8 Draft Taps

Situated in the centre of a plaza, the Ivy is a flight of steps down from street level. The bar has plenty of dartboards and a pool table. A separate banquet room with a capacity of 60 is available for private parties. The menu is mainly pub fare with daily specials. During the hockey season the bar puts on many specials including wings and draft nights. Entertainment is provided every Friday night and is a mixture of live music and karaoke; call for details. Big screen for all sporting events, including satellite.

O'Malley's

Address: 8 Queen Street East, Brampton
Telephone: 905-453-8300
Proprietor: Hoa Lee
Opened: 1979
Bar: 14 Draft Taps

Set in a century building originally built in 1888 as a police station, this pub is one of a few in Ontario that are reputedly haunted. Many regulars and staff have seen the ghostly image of a man walking the length of the bar and then disappearing. Kelly behind the bar is one of these people and is willing to share her tale with you. A big screen for all sporting events and a darts area. Traditional pub fare menu, with Monday being jug and wing night. Entertainment at weekends is mainly karaoke but periodical live bands are featured; please call for details.

❖

McGonagalls

Address: 431c St. Paul Avenue, Brantford
Telephone: 519-759-5480
Proprietors: Ann and Dave Dodds
Opened: 1993
Bar: 12 Draft Taps

Tartan carpet and tartan seat covers are the first giveaway that you are in Brantford's authentic Scottish pub. Owner Dave is soccer crazy and the walls have a great collection of shirts from all over Britain, as well as other memorabilia, including old game programs and photographs of Dave's beloved Dundee United. A large-screen TV for all major soccer games and a table-top football game round out this football fan's dream rec room. A good selection of single malts and a traditional pub fare menu with a Scottish flair. Trivia night is every Tuesday.

Purdy's Pub

Address: 89 Colborne Street East, Brantford
Telephone: 519-750-0955
Proprietor: Bryant Purdy
Opened: 2000
Bar: 16 Draft Taps

A long narrow pub with a 40-foot sit-down bar running down the left side and two large booths at the end. A popular place due to both the excellent food and close proximity to the casino. When parking round back patrons have to take the old freight elevator up four flights; on special nights don't be surprised to find a uniformed operator. The large traditional menu is mostly homemade, from the burgers right down to the fries. Monday to Friday Purdy's has a rapid lunch where as it's 20 minutes or free. Monday is a two-for-one wings special, Wednesday has two-for-one fish and chips and Friday and Saturday it's a prime rib dinner. Entertainment every weekend.

❖

Whistler's Pub

Address: 214 King George Road, Brantford
Telephone: 519-720-0010
Proprietors: Ray and Janet
Opened: 2001
Bar: 5 Draft Taps

A very traditional English pub with a host hailing from Bromley, Kent, and a chef who comes from Greenwich. Don't let the draft choices fool you, as Ray keeps 27 varieties of British beers in bottles and cans. There is a piano in the bar for a good old-fashioned singalong. Devonshire cream teas with scones and strawberry jam are served daily from 2 PM to 4 PM. The menu is very traditional with an English flair and most meals are homemade daily in house. A big favourite is the deluxe ploughman's lunch with a mixture of imported cheeses. Friday has a fish and chips special, while Sunday features a traditional roast beef dinner. English trivia on Wednesday nights and entertainment at the weekend.

❖

The Keystorm

Address: 2 Courthouse Avenue, Brockville
Telephone: 613-345-0404
Proprietor: Louise
Opened: 2000
Bar: 11 Draft Taps

Named after the S.S. Keystorm that sank in the St. Lawrence in 1912 and is now a popular dive site, the Keystorm is situated in a building steeped in history. At the turn of the century it housed the pharmaceutical Fulford Company which made millions from their worldwide mail order of "Pink pills for Pale people." In 1958 the building was home to the Brockville Trust and Loan Company when it became the scene of Canada's biggest bank robbery, with over $3^{1}/2 million stolen. The original bank vault today is now the beer cooler, complete with the original safe door. The pub is open everyday at 7:30 AM for breakfast and the menu is a good cross-section featuring traditional Irish fare, pizzas and pasta. Highly recommended are the Dublin-cut lamb chops. Live bands perform Thursday, Friday and Saturday evenings and also Sunday afternoons. A popular pub with divers in summer.

❖

The Isaac Brock

Address: 59 King Street West, Brockville
Telephone: 613-342-7860
Proprietors: Three brothers from Manchester
Opened: 1982
Bar: 10 Draft Taps

A long sit-down bar is the focal point of this classy British-style pub. A large separate and beautifully furnished non-smoking dining room is at the rear of the pub. Booths line the far wall in the bar area. At the time of writing renovations were under way to add a patio and walk outdoors from the bar. A separate dart area with four boards. The menu is varied with a mix of traditional and a wide variety of burgers, but the claim of the bar is that they have the best fish and chips not only in town but also in Ontario. A separate kids' menu, and the Thursday night special is a prime rib dinner. Entertainment on special occasions; please call for details.

Burlington

The Black Bull

Address: 1124 Guelph Line, Burlington
Telephone: 905-332-4922
Proprietor: Dennis Dupuis
Opened: 1987
Bar: 13 Draft Taps

This club-like bar has a separate games room with two pool tables and dartboards. It is also home to the Burlington Glasgow Rangers supporters club and shows all Rangers games in the large banquet room. The banquet room can also be booked for private parties. The menu is mostly traditional fare with the general consensus of the regulars that the fish and chips are the best in Burlington. Wednesday is all day and night wing specials. Thursday is fish and chip night and Friday to Sunday it's the prime rib special, where for a little more money but a lot more food there's the popular Black Bull cut. Entertainment is karaoke Wednesday to Saturday and the Black Bull is the *Burlington Post* readers' choice for best karaoke bar in Burlington four years in a row.

The Dickens
Address: 423 Elizabeth Street, Burlington
Telephone: 905-333-4991
Proprietor: Mike Dickson
Opened: 1988
Bar: 12 Draft Taps
Situated in the picturesque Burlington village square this well-known pub has a couple of dining areas including one with a large window looking out to the patio, giving an atrium effect. The menu is a good cross-section of traditional pub fare and appetizers along with in-house favourites like the exceptional curried seafood. Entertainment every Saturday and Sunday evenings, with arguably the best pub band in Ontario, 3MDM, playing alternate Sundays.

The Judge and Jury
Address: 1222 Walkers Line, Burlington
Telephone: 905-319-1655
Proprietors: Andy, Mark and Kevin
Opened: 1998
Bar: 17 Draft Taps
Across from a large hockey arena, this pub is a popular hangout for hockey teams and was voted the *Burlington Post* readers' choice pub of the year three years in a row. Three dartboards available in the bar. The menu is a good cross-section of traditional fare and a great selection of pizza and calzones. Saturdays, Sundays and holidays the bar features breakfast specials. Located in a large plaza there is plenty of parking. Entertainment periodical; please call for details.

❖

The Plough and Harrow
Address: 3040 New Street, Burlington
Telephone: 905-634-4552
Manager: Donna Bell
Opened: 1986
Bar: 13 Draft Taps

One of the oldest British-style pubs in town, it is not unusual to find the bar engaged in a spontaneous sing-song as it is the hang-out of the world-renowned Male Orpheus Choir. The bar is also very soccer-oriented and shows all the major games on the big screen. A staple of the pub is the showing of *Coronation Street* every day at 3 PM Monday to Thursday. The menu has a large selection of traditional pub fare with exceptional homemade pies. Monday is wing night and Friday features fish and chips. Sundays prove to be popular for the big British breakfast fan. Entertainment every Saturday night and an open-entry pub quiz every other Thursday.

The Queen's Head
Address: 400 Brant Street, Burlington
Telephone: 905-632-1300
Proprietor: Josie
Opened: 1995
Bar: 14 Draft Taps

A very authentic British pub with a great selection of historical pictures and old British newspaper headlines covering the walls. The bar contains dartboards and a big-screen TV for all sporting events. A good selection of single malts available. The menu is mainly traditional with an excellent array of finger foods, including the popular Singapore pot stickers. A large special coffees list, with the Braveheart coffee proving to be a real favourite. Karaoke on Thursday and Saturday evenings, with big prizes every six weeks. During the winter months trivia nights are held on Mondays. The bar also has an adjoining fine dining restaurant called the Annapolis Grill.

The Slye Fox

Address: 4057 New Street, Burlington
Telephone: 905-639-3900
Proprietor: John Anderson
Opened: 1999
Bar: 20 Draft Taps

This large open bar has a dedicated darts area and a games room which includes a shuffleboard table. At the long sit-down bar to the left as you walk in you will find a regular clientele from all walks of life. The large menu is a mix of traditional and North American fare with excellent daily specials and the following evening specials: Monday — Wings; Tuesday — Two-for-one fish and chips; Wednesday — Two-for-one pasta; Sunday — Prime rib dinner. In the summer Wednesday nights feature an east coast kitchen party with special menu and east coast bands; call for details. Live bands every Friday and Saturday evening and also one Tuesday of each month features a blues night with well-known recording artists. Wednesday night is also an open-entry pub quiz that is proving to be very popular.

The Winchester Arms

Address: 450 Appleby Line, Burlington
Telephone: 905-634-0363
General Manager: Michelle Bradley
Opened: 1992
Bar: 12 Draft Taps

This cozy bar with its Victorian-style décor specializes in freshly-made-on-the-premises lunch menu. The sit-down bar is busy in the early evening with a loyal clientele who have been there from day one. A dartboard section is at the back of the bar. The menu is traditional/North American mix with the following evening specials: Tuesday — Half-price appetizers; Wednesday — Wings; Friday — Fish and chips; Saturday: Steak specials. Entertainment on St.Patrick's Day is all-day, with a special Irish menu complementing the annual packed party.

The Caledon Inn

Address: 16626 Airport Road, Caledon East
Telephone: 905-584-5202
Proprietor: Keith Crossgrove

The majestic Caledon Inn sits in 25 acres of woodland containing walking and cross-country ski trails, many hooking up with the Trans Canada Trail. The building dates back to the early 1800s and the little pub downstairs still has its original stone walls. Wooden beams and floors along with the cozy fireplace add to the feeling that you have stepped back in time to a traditional country pub. The large outdoor patio has a full-service gazebo bar and a tented area in case of rain. The pub encourages families to bring the kids, as a large front garden is the perfect spot for them to run around while you sit back and relax on the patio. Many patrons take advantage of the trails then return to the pub for a pint and a bite to eat. Upstairs at the inn is a fine dining room, while another floor above is available for small groups complete with its own balcony. The pub has its own menu featuring traditional fare with the upstairs menu available as well. Weekly Thursday sessions feature the best of local musicians while Wednesday night rotates between blues and jazz. Occasional weekend entertainment; call for details.

Cambridge

The Black Badger

Address: 55 Water Street North, Cambridge
Telephone: 519-624-0892
Proprietors: Marissa and Tom Silcock
Opened: 1996
Bar: 15 Draft Taps

Located on the Grand River in the historical downtown area of Galt, this authentic Tudor-style pub offers a great menu and excellent selection of imported and domestic draft beer. Some of the signature items offered on the menu include sizzling 'shrooms, steak-and-Guinness pie, and liver and onions. Daily lunch and dinner specials. A dart room is located on the second floor. Entertainment every other Saturday features the best of local talent. The small roadside patio is a very popular summer spot offering a good blend of sun and shade.

❖

Burn's Howff

Address: 95 Saginaw Parkway, Cambridge
Telephone: 519-622-6671
Proprietors: Norrie and Sean
Opened: 1995
Bar: 14 Draft Taps

This pub has a definite Scottish flair — one only has to note the décor and the limited-edition print of Robert the Bruce in action at Bannockburn hanging on the wall. The bar has a pool table and a table-top football game along with dartboards. The bar shows all major soccer games on the big screen. A good selection of single malts with one being showcased weekly. The menu features such favourites as fish and chips, and the regulars state that the wings are the best in Cambridge. Entertainment weekly, with Sunday nights hosting a jam session.

Fiddle and Firkin

Address: 707 King Street East, Cambridge
Telephone: 519-653-8835
Proprietor: Jerry Quigg
Bar: 16 Draft Taps

Situated in the heart of Cambridge, the Fiddle offers a cozy non-smoking family atmosphere. The small sit-down bar is at the rear of the pub and a small patio sits out front. Voted "Best British Pub" in Cambridge for the year 2000, the pub boasts a talented chef and attentive staff. The menu is a good mix of traditional and North American fare with many daily specials. The pub has a couple of dartboards and every Wednesday night hosts a pub quiz that is an open entry.

❖

Fiddlers Green
Address: 121/2 Water Street South, Cambridge
Telephone: 519-622-5270
Proprietor: Nash Cohen
Opened: 1998
Bar: 18 Draft Taps

This Irish pub/night club is situated in the famous Galt post office building, which was designed by Canadian architect Thomas Fuller who created Canada's first parliament buildings that were destroyed by fire in 1916. The pub has two large patio decks overlooking the Grand River, including one which is at least 50 feet up. The main floor bar has large windows adding to the view. There is also a centre stage where many well-known rock bands are booked regularly. The second floor is a dance bar with disc jockey and is open at weekends. The third floor attic has a private lounge complete with a waterfall bar, track lighting and an aquarium; this lounge can be hired for private parties. The pub is one of the most famous haunted sites in Canada and the ghost of Emily has been seen by staff and patrons alike. The private lounge is in the old clock tower and it is here that Emily hung herself due to a tragic love affair with the town's postmaster at the turn of the last century. At midnight it is the custom to raise a glass to Emily's ghost. The food at the Fiddlers is outstanding and was voted in 2000 by the Cambridge Chamber of Commerce as the best casual dining in town.

❖

The Golden Kiwi Pub
Address: 14 Petty Place, Cambridge
Telephone: 519-622-3722
Proprietors: Len and Judie Owens
Opened: 1990
Telephone: 13 Draft Taps

Owners Len and Judie are pride in their New Zealand heritage and it is reflected in the style and décor of this cozy corner pub. Once a year the Kiwi brings in Maori dancers and the show is a sell-out. A large selection of New Zealand and Australian wines results in frequent wine tastings. The pub also has an excellent collection of single malts and Scotch tastings are done as well; please call for details. The draft beers include local micro breweries and the fridge is also stocked with New Zealand beers. Three menus are available — lunch, dinner and late night — and all are a cosmopolitan mix. There are weekly fish, pasta and curry specials, with the coconut chicken curry with pecan and almonds the definite favourite. Entertainment every second Sunday from September until June, featuring a Celtic jam session.

Carp

The Cheshire Cat
Address: 2193 Richardson Side Road, Carp
Telephone: 613-831-2183/**Web:** http://www.kirkstonehouse.com
Proprietors: Christine Totti and Bob Hargrave
Opened: 1989
Bar: 11 Draft Taps

Built to replace an old log schoolhouse, this stone structure was erected in 1883 and remained a school until 1957. During renovations to build the pub in 1989, original ceiling boards were discovered and are now the downstairs interior walls. A traditional dinner menu along with a separate lunch and late-night snack menu are available. A small non-smoking dining room with seating for 30 is upstairs. Daily happy hour munchies between 4 PM and 6 PM includes the popular mussels-and-a-pint deal. The pub also runs a small bed and breakfast in a neighbouring stone cottage.

❖

The Swan at Carp

Address: 108 Falldown Lane, Carp
Telephone: 613-839-7926/**Web:** http://www.theswanatcarp.com
Proprietors: Stan Dugdale and Anita Nadeau
Opened: 1987
Bar: 9 Draft Taps

Landlord Stan takes his draft beers seriously and includes in his selection a mixture of cask-conditioned real ales and local breweries; twice a year the Carp hosts eagerly anticipated beer tastings. The pub itself was originally a Presbyterian manse and sits halfway up the well-named Falldown Lane. The pub also has regular malt tastings as well as wine and port. The Cygnet Ring is the name given to patrons who attend these tastings and during the course of the year they raise large amounts of money for the Canadian Guide Dogs for the Blind Association. The menu is traditional and features a roast beef carvery every Sunday between 11 AM and 2 PM. The Carp features the best of live jazz two Fridays of every month, except once a month in July and August.

King George Inn

Address: 77 Albert Street, Cobourg
Telephone: 905-377-9971
General Manager: Mark Melvin
Opened: 1999
Bar: 13 Draft Taps

The Victoria and Albert Pub is located in the old King George Inn, which was once the Cobourg jail. This original Inn was made into a jail in 1902. In 1998 it reverted to its present inn status, but a lot of the original cells are still standing in the pub; even the washrooms are separated by the old cell bars. There is also a small museum in the solitary confinement area. The Inn upstairs has many beautiful rooms overlooking Lake Ontario. Each room has its own distinctive style and name, including the Warden's Keep and the Privileged Prisoner. The pub has a play area for kids, allowing parents to enjoy a few moments' relaxation. The pub menu is traditional pub fare and more. Monday is wing night and Saturday it's the prime rib special. The patio offers a superb view of the lake, especially the annual tall ships festival. For that special dinner there is fine dining in the aptly named Warden's Table.

Collingwood

The Admiral's Post

Address: 2 Schoolhouse Lane, Collingwood
Telephone: 705-445-1833
Proprietor: Leanne Calvert
Opened: 1995
Bar: 12 Draft Taps

Located in a century-old home in the heart of Collingwood, this English-style pub is popular with tourists during summer and the winter skiing months. The small sit-down bar is to the right as you walk in and a small snug section is at the rear of the dining area. Dartboards and a big-screen TV for all major sporting events. A good selection of single malts and wines are available. The menu is varied, including a large traditional fare section. The evening specials are as follows: Monday — Pasta; Tuesday — Fish and chips; Wednesday — Wings; Thursday — Schnitzel; Friday and Saturday: Lamb dinner; Sunday — two-for-one roast beef dinners. Entertainment periodical, so please call for details.

❖

Molly Bloom's

Address: 27 Simcoe Street, Collingwood
Telephone: 705-445-0442
Manager: Andrea
Opened: 1999
Bar: 11 Draft Taps

Large oak beams and wooden plank floors coupled with the continuous background Irish music give this bar an authentic pub feel. Monday nights are movie nights on the big screen along with free popcorn. The menu is a traditional/North American mix with Friday evenings being all-you-can-eat fish and chips. Wings are on special nightly after 8 PM and a large Sunday breakfast is served from 9 AM until 2 PM. Entertainment on Tuesday night by d.j. Lenny and live bands perform Wednesday to Saturday nights. Don't be surprised if you see Elvis sitting at the bar drinking a pint of Guinness during the annual Elvis festival held the last weekend of July in Collingwood.

❖

The Waltzing Weasel
Address: 1437 King Street East, Courtice
Telephone: 905-404-0251
Proprietor: Jennifer "Sam" Moyle
Opened: 2000
Bar: 22 Draft Taps

The interior of this unique-shaped building is a mixture of wood and brick with lots of large arched windows that add a touch of grandeur to the décor. Two upper dining areas are at opposite ends of the room, while the sit-down bar is located in the middle. Two gas fireplaces add to the charm. Sam believes in promoting a friendly atmosphere and for this the staff are regularly rewarded with prizes, such as cash and trips. The menu is a good mixture of traditional fare and much more, with most items being made from scratch on the premises.

Dundas

The Prickly Thistle
Address: 93 King Street West, Dundas
Telephone: 905-627-4410
Proprietor: John McManus
Opened: 2001
Bar: 13 Draft Taps

Scottish-style pub with pictures and posters of Scottish themes covering most walls. A long 40-foot sit-down bar runs down one side of the pub and then the bar drops a level to the stage and dance floor areas. A large banquet room is available for private functions and also hosts the Thistle's annual New Year's Eve party where celebrations start at 7 PM to bring in the Scottish new year. The menu is a traditional/North American mix with many evening specials that change monthly and include fajitas, steak, roast beef, curry, and wing and pizza nights. Karaoke on Thursdays and live bands Friday and Saturday.

❖

The Winchester Arms

Address: 120 King Street West, Dundas
Telephone: 905-627-8016
Proprietor: Rick Paddock
Opened: 1993
Bar: 17 Draft Taps

This narrow bar is large contrary to deceptive outside impressions, mainly because of the large room at the back which contains dartboards and a pinball machine. This room can be booked free of charge for private functions. The upper level is lined with booths that are separated from the bar by open bookshelves. The menu is large and contains many traditional pub fare dishes as well as the following evening specials: Monday — Fish and chips; Tuesday — All you can eat wings; Thursday — Curry; Saturday: Steak night. Breakfast is available Saturdays and Sundays from 10 AM until 3 PM. Entertainment periodical; please call for details.

Elora

The Shepherd's Crook

Address: 8 Mill Street West, Elora
Telephone: 519-846-5775
Proprietor: Richard Ruggle
Opened: 1997
Bar: 13 Draft Taps

Sitting at the back of this pub, you are offered a spectacular close-up view of the Grand River as it flows by on its journey south. A large upstairs section of this 100-year-old building is designated non-smoking. The bar has four micro brews, including Elora Irish ales. The menu is traditional pub fare with many daily specials. The bar is at its busiest during the annual Elora Music Festival, which runs the last week of July. An Irish busker provides the entertainment Saturday and Sunday afternoons. The Elora Gorge is not too far away and this pub makes the perfect resting or meeting point.

The Rob Roy Inn

Address: 156 Main Street, Erin
Telephone: 519-833-0639
Proprietor: Dan McLaughlin
Opened: 1999
Bar: 9 Draft Taps

Erin is located among the beautiful Caledon Hills by the forks of the Credit River, famous for its trout fishing. After a day's fishing or sight seeing, what better way to relax than in the majestic Rob Roy. This building dates back to 1886 and for a long time was the village doctor's surgery. The owner, Dan from Kirkintilloch in Scotland, is an accomplished carpenter and built the bar himself. There is a non-smoking dining room that is reminiscent of an old Victorian tea room. A large games lounge has pool tables and a fireplace with a portrait of Rob Roy proudly hanging above. The inn also has plenty of accommodation available. An old piano sits in the pub and if you can play it Dan will accompany you on his accordion. The menu is mainly pub fare with daily specials. Entertainment periodical; call for details.

❖

Badger and Firkin

Address: 555 Burnhamthorpe Road, Etobicoke
Telephone: 416-620-5959
Proprietor: Glen Woodcock
Opened: 1998
Bar: 16 Draft Taps

Conveniently located on Burnhamthorpe, one stop west of the 427. The Badger has a large bar area which includes a pool table and big-screen TV. A separate and comfortable non-smoking dining room is available and this section also includes a dart area. The layout is a mix of tables and booths with carpeting throughout and red upholstery. A large 40-foot patio sits out front. The Badger has over eight TVs and a satellite system to show most major sporting events. NTN trivia is always at the bar. The menu is very varied with many daily specials. Wings are on special every Saturday, Sunday and Monday.

The Galway Arms

Address: 838 The Queensway, Etobicoke
Telephone: 416-251-0096
Proprietor: Tommy Keane
Opened: 1991
Bar: 12 Draft Taps

A very traditional Irish pub with all the staff Irish-born and the majority of the customers from Ireland as well. The Irish counties association have their pub nights here. The Galway shows a lot of Gaelic games at the weekend and when they are on, the place is packed to the doors. The sit-down bar is in the centre of the room and serves both the lounge and bar area. The menu is homemade traditional fare with the kitchen closing at 5 PM daily, except Sundays when the special is roast beef and Belfast ham from 3:30 until late. The biggest St. Patrick's Day party around with first come, first served. Entertainment every Friday and Saturday night features traditional Irish bands.

Fox and Fiddle

Address: 171 Carlingview, Etobicoke
Telephone: 416-798-3203
General Manager: Bill Ganas
Opened: 1992
Bar: 24 Draft Taps

This pub is right next to Pearson Airport and makes an excellent pre-flight meeting place or a place to unwind after a long trip. The large dining area has a central brick-surround fireplace and there is a separate games area with the popular golf game and pay-as-you-go internet hook-up. There are plenty of booths in the bar including a few just for couples. A large south-facing patio catches the sun all day. The large menu is a great mix of North American and traditional dishes and the appetizers are half-price Monday to Friday between 4 PM and 6 PM. Wings are on special Monday and Tuesday evenings. This bar does a great lunch-time trade with its popular lunch specials. Karaoke every Friday night.

Fox and Fiddle

Address: 3473 Lakeshore Boulevard West, Etobicoke
Telephone: 416-255-4126
General Manager: Bill Lykardopoulos
Opened: 2001
Bar: 24 Draft Taps

The downstairs of this bar has three pool tables and plenty of dart-boards and is also the place to be most evenings, with entertainment five nights a week. Tuesday has an open jam session, Thursday and Friday it's the latest sounds with the house disc jockey, Saturday features the best in live entertainment, and Sunday you can win cash prizes by trying your luck at karaoke. The upstairs bar has a large dining area and a long sit-down bar. The menu features many daily specials including Sunday afternoons when the nachos are two-for-one. Wings are on special Mondays from 10 PM to close. Tuesday is wings and draft night, Wednesday get two-for-one fajitas. Thursday night is ladies' night at the bar. Chase the Fox specials at the bar daily; ask your server for details.

Fox and Fiddle

Address: 4946 Dundas Street West, Etobicoke
Telephone: 416-207-9990
General Manager: Theresa Di Nardo
Opened: 2000
Bar: 22 Draft Taps

Red velvet seating and carpet throughout give this pub a very traditional English look. An open area at the front then narrows past the long sit-down bar before opening on to a large back room containing a pool table and giant pull-down TV screen which then leads out to the large back patio deck. The menu features many favourites and has the following specials: Monday — Buffalo chicken chunks; Tuesday — Wings, and Saturday and Sunday the ever-popular 10-oz. prime rib dinner with Yorkshire pudding. Wings are also on special every Saturday evening between 10 PM and close. Live entertainment every Thursday, which is when the ladies receive 50 percent off entrees. Friday there's a disc jockey and the chance to win a television, while Saturday also has a disc jockey and a chance to win one hundred dollars.

❖

The Rose and Thorne
Address: 1100 Islington Avenue, Etobicoke
Telephone: 416-233-8827
Proprietor: Anne Louise Hall
Opened: 1995
Bar: 13 Draft Taps

This Nova Scotian pub with its nautical décor has all the warmth and friendliness one associates with the east coast. Comfortable seating and a gas fireplace in the upper section make for a cozy night. This pub was voted by a local newspaper's readers the best in Etobicoke for the years 2000 and 2001. A splendid surprise is the backyard patio which looks out onto a small green area. The menu is traditional with a definite Nova Scotia feel with plenty of seafood specials. At the time of writing the Rose was working on a full-time oyster bar. Entertainment every Thursday, Friday and Saturday evenings consisting of traditional east coast music.

The Shamrock and Thistle
Address: 4923 Dundas Street West, Etobicoke
Telephone: 416-239-9468
Proprietors: Audrey, Michael and Mick
Opened: 1998
Bar:

When you mix the Celtic races of Scottish and Irish this is probably what you would get — a friendly neighbourhood pub with plenty of both in it. The long sit-down bar zig zags from the front of the pub to halfway down the left side. A dining section at the back with a small non-smoking alcove is where you will find the big screen that shows all sporting events, especially soccer and N.F.L. The pub has wooden floors and the walls are covered in Scottish and Irish memorabilia. The menu is very traditional and includes the likes of Scotch broth. Food specials are done in conjunction with televised sports events, especially on Sundays during football season. Just ask Kristina behind the bar, as she is the pub's resident sports guru.

Scruffy Murphy's
Address: 225 The East Mall, Etobicoke
Telephone: 416-231-9411
Proprietor: Andy Hicki-Szabo
Opened: 2001
Bar: 16 Draft Taps

This elegant Irish pub is tastefully decorated with Irish prints and memorabilia. There are several separate dining areas, including one with a granite fireplace over which hangs a large image of a Celtic tiger. The pub is named after an Irish immigrant who left Ireland because of the great famine, and his wanderlust is reflected in the varied international menu. The food is of the highest quality and many daily specials are featured; a weekend brunch is also available. A small room off to the side of the bar known as "The Library" contains a pool table. A Celtic jam every Wednesday and live bands on Friday and Saturdays.

The Squire and Firkin
Address: 3335 Bloor Street West, Etobicoke
Telephone: 416-233-6531
Proprietor: Kate
Opened: 1996
Bar: 16 Draft Taps

This pub is perfect for those who like to enjoy a little privacy, as the pub has many nooks and crannies with plenty of booths. At the back you will find dartboards and a pool table. The windows slide open to the streetside patio. There's a large pull-down TV screen for the big games. Pull a seat up at the bar for the N.T.N. trivia game. The menu has a mix including traditional fare, with an excellent selection of daily specials. Wings are on special every day. Tuesday night is karaoke and Thursday is casino night at no cost to enter and plenty of prizes. The last Sunday of every month is jam night.

Tessie McDaids

Address: 5078 Dundas Street West, Etobicoke
Telephone: 416-207-1111
Proprietors: Theresa and Kenneth
Opened: 1999
Bar: 8 Draft Taps

A traditional Irish pub with plenty of Irish posters and prints. The bar is small with bench seating around the perimeter of the little room. A large Guinness mirror takes up one wall and a collection of soccer shirts hangs on the others. A side patio is covered halfway by a vine-laden trellis and a small bar sits at the end of it. The menu is homemade Irish pub fare and Fridays, weather permitting, there's a barbecue on the patio. Entertainment is periodical, but St. Patrick's Day sees an all-day party featuring Irish country dancers and live music.

Fergus

The Ferguson Room
Address: 478 St. Andrews Street West, Fergus
Telephone: 519-843-4770
Proprietors: Joe and Peter Egger
Opened: 1996
Bar: 10 Draft Taps

A part of the historical Breadalbane Inn, this small, cozy pub has a small sit-down bar with a good selection of single malts and micro brewery drafts. The inn was originally a stone cottage built in the 1850s before it was enlarged in 1879 to the building it is now. There is an adjoining fine dining restaurant with an extensive wine list. Twelve rooms are available at the inn for accommodation. The pub menu includes many traditional dishes as well as an excellent curry. The bar has a small dining area with a library backdrop.

The Highlander Inn
Address: 280 Bridge Street, Fergus
Telephone: 519-843-3115
General Manager: Eileen McLaughlin
Opened: 1989
Bar: 9 Draft Taps

A small pub with a large adjoining dining room and a larger bar downstairs called the Andy Capp Room. The small pub was hand-built by Eileen's father Dan, who also owns the Rob Roy in Erin. Very popular place during the Fergus Highland Games and the seven rooms available are always booked well in advance. The menu is varied with a definite Scottish flair. Entertainment every second Friday, and during the highland games the pub features the popular Scottish duo the Nicky Tams. Burns' Night at the Highlander is always a sell-out and customers are advised to get their tickets early. A favourite overnight stay with fishermen, as Fergus is close to many well-known fly fishing streams.

The Fox and Duke

Address: 9619 Highway 15, Franktown
Telephone: 613-283-4895
Proprietors: Richard Carter and Eleanor Placquet
Opened: 1998
Bar: 10 Draft Taps

Located just east of Perth on Highway 7, then south on Highway 15, the village of Franktown is the lilac capital of Ontario with an annual festival the last week of May. The pub was named after the Duke of Richmond, the head of the British troops in Canada who unfortunately met his untimely death after being bitten by a rabid fox not far from the pub's present site. The pub has been well chronicled in view of the fact that it is haunted by several ghosts, including a previous reformed alcoholic owner who stated that no liquor would ever again be served on the premises. The opening of the Fox seemingly has caused his reappearance and he is not happy. The place was built by Scottish stonemasons in 1830 while over here to work on the Rideau Canal. The menu is Canadian fare with a few traditional items. A banquet room is available for private parties.

❖

Georgetown

The George and Dragon
Address: 7 Main Street North, Georgetown
Telephone: 905-873-4459
Proprietor: Julie Yake
Opened: 1989
Bar: 13 Draft Taps

This pub is an impressive building that sits on its own large lot. Traditional English décor inside with a large open snug to the right of the bar. A separate dart area is perfect for the teams that play out of the George. The menu is varied with a large traditional pub fare section; a daily menu is placed on each table highlighting the specials and includes a low-fat selection. A prime rib special is available Friday, Saturday and Sunday. A favourite is the large British breakfast for the hearty appetite. A jazz band plays on the last Sunday afternoon of each month.

Glen Williams

The Copper Kettle Pub
Address: 517 Main Street, Glen Williams
Telephone: 905-877-5551
Proprietors: Graham and Brenda Gove
Opened: 1987
Bar: 9 Draft Taps

An old general store that has not been changed since it was built in 1825. Because of this, it is highly sought after by film crews, causing the pub to temporarily close its doors once in a while. One of the store employees was a young Timothy Eaton who learned his trade here before moving on to bigger things. The interior of the pub is in keeping with the exterior and includes an old piano circa 1840 and furniture made from local reclaimed wood. A small patio to the side of the pub has the soothing sounds of running water and is often used for wedding photos with its picture-perfect background. A fireplace sits in the bar and its surround is a replica of the front of the building. Graham and his family are only to glad to share the history of this one-of-a-kind pub with you. The traditional menu is all homemade and cooked in the small store kitchen. Glen Williams is just a mile or so north of Georgetown from Highway 7.

❖

Molly Bloom's

Address: 91 Wyndham Street, Guelph
Telephone: 519-823-0159
Manager: Elsie Hart
Opened: 1999
Bar: 16 Draft Taps

This Irish-style pub, although fairly new on the block, is fast becoming a student favourite, mainly because of the growing popularity of live Celtic music, which is featured in Molly Bloom's Thursday, Friday and Saturday evenings. Tuesday nights also see an open jam session. A small upper section with a couple of tables at the front window look out onto downtown Guelph. A large-screen TV features all sports. The menu is a mixture of traditional fare and a selection of sandwiches and wraps. Wings are on special Monday nights and two-for-one burgers are featured Monday to Thursday nights.

The Penny Whistle

Address: 2 Quebec Street, Guelph
Telephone: 519-836-4792
Proprietor: Satish Thukral
Opened: 1995
Bar: 18 Draft Taps

English-style pub with traditional décor. Three dartboards to one side of the pub and a large-screen TV in the centre of the bar area. A small dining section at the far end of the bar. This pub is famous for its curry, with over 16 varieties. Satish took a trip back to Manchester and when he saw how popular curry was becoming in Britain he decided to put it to the test here in Canada and it works. The curries range from mild to the very hot vindaloos. The most popular night of the week is Thursdays when from 6 PM until 11 PM the Penny puts on an all-you-can-eat curry buffet, the ultimate feast for curry lovers. The menu also has more traditional choices ranging from Cornish pasties to a ploughman's lunch. Friday and Saturday from 5 PM to 10 PM the special is prime rib dinner. Entertainment on St. Patrick's Day all day.

❖

Shakespeare Arms
Address: 35 Harvard Road, Guelph
Telephone: 519-767-6003
Proprietor: Terry Chuchmach
Opened: 1992
Bar: 21 Draft Taps

This is a charming Tudor-style building with an interior of black beams and red English traditional pub carpet. There is a large brick fireplace in the bar area with a portrait of the bard himself hanging above it. The dart section is set apart from the rest of the bar and has its own little lounge. The fixtures in the pub and most of the memorabilia were brought over from England in the 70s. The menu is varied with traditional pub fare and a late night section. Evening specials are as follows: Monday — Wing night; Tuesday — Kids eat free; Thursday — Rib night; Friday — Fish and chips; Sunday — Roast beef dinner. Entertainment Thursday, Friday and Saturday nights.

The Sherlock Holmes
Address: 76 Baker Street, Guelph
Telephone: 519-766-0222
Proprietor: Colt Archer
Opened: 1997
Bar: 16 Draft Taps

A friendly neighbourhood pub with a large British Isles clientele. Big-screen TV for all major soccer games. An enclosed snug leads off from the small downstairs bar. Upstairs has a pool table and dartboards as well as live entertainment and a d.j. at the weekends. The menu is very traditional with specials as follows: Monday — Fish and chips; Wednesday — Curry; Sunday — Roast beef. Wings are on special on the nights in between. Deep-fried Mars bars round out the menu.

The Woolwich Arms and Arrow

Address: 176 Woolwich Street, Guelph
Telephone: 519-836-2875
Proprietor: Bob Desautels
Opened: 1990
Bar: 15 Draft Taps

A uniquely Canadian pub, the concept behind the Arrow group is to offer and promote local micro-brewed beers, wines and locally produced food. A totally "buy local" philosophy ensures fresher product and more often than not better prices. Affectionately known as the Woolie, the pub sits in a century-old home with a patio out front and back. Many of the draft beers are cask-conditioned and micro breweries. Beer tastings are frequent in the Woolie as they strive to promote the local breweries. The pub also has a good selection of single malts and Scotch tastings are also done throughout the year. The menu is varied and each item that is marked with the trillium means that all ingredients were sourced exclusively in Ontario. The Tuesday special is curry, Wednesday is British Isle fare, Thursday is a vegetable delight and Friday is the Chef's Roast.

Haliburton

Gunners Pub

Address: Sir Sam's Inn, Eagle Lake, Haliburton
Telephone: 705-754-2188
Innkeeper: James T. Orr
Opened: 1965
Bar: 4 Draft Taps

Highway 11 to Highway 118 east to Eagle Lake Road 2 then follow signs to Sir Sam's Inn. Situated on breathtaking Eagle Lake, the Gunners Pub is more of an amenity for overnight guests but visitors to the area are welcome. A cozy little pub with a dartboard, pool table and shuffleboard at your disposal. The pub has a soup-and-sandwich lunch. Sir Sam's Inn has 16 lakeside accommodations and in the summer is a great base for water skiing, windsurfing, sailing, kayaking or canoeing. If water sports are not your thing then there is a great nature trail for trekking or mountain biking. Cross country and downhill skiing available in winter. The Inn also has a conference wing and what better way to finish the day than with a couple of pints in the Gunners. The pub is closed mid November until December 27 and also the month of April.

Hamilton

The Cat 'n' Fiddle

Address: 174 John Street South, Hamilton
Telephone: 905-525-3855
Proprietor: Reg Collett
Opened: 1993
Bar: 12 Draft Taps

A very traditional English-style pub with authentic décor and memorabilia. You see the bar area as you walk in with a lounge on the other side. A back room contains a big screen for sporting events, which keeps the noise away from the rest of the pub. A separate darts area makes up the rest of the pub. The menu is very traditional and is available until midnight with the following specials: Monday — Two-for-one dinners; Wednesday — Wings; Thursday — Burgers; Friday — Fish and chips. Saturday and Sundays have terrific dinner special — maybe lamb, prime rib or chicken with all the trimmings. One of the more popular choices is the all-day breakfast special and for many the best bargain in town.

❖

Dodger and Firkin

Address: 2255 Barton Street East, Unit 11, Hamilton
Telephone: 905-573-7430
Proprietor: Terry Yates
Opened: 1999
Bar: 16 Draft Taps

The Dodger is an old-style English pub with a large sit-down bar in front of you as you enter the front door. A games area runs up one side with two pool tables and two Golden Tee golf games. An enclosed darts section is great for league games. The upstairs is a non-smoking dining room and can also be booked for private parties. A secluded patio makes a great backdrop to a quiet summertime pint. The menu features many great daily specials. Wings are on special Thursday nights and there are Firkin Friday deals at the bar between 3 and 5 P.M., while a traditional prime rib dinner is featured on Saturday. Thursday night is ladies' night at the Dodger and at the time of writing a singles night is in the works; please call for details. Live bands every Saturday night.

The Gown and Gavel

Address: 24 Hess Street South, Hamilton
Telephone: 905-523-8881/**E-mail:** hessvillag@msn.com
Proprietor: Bruce New
Opened: 1981
Bar: 10 Draft Taps

Set in the trendy Hess Village with a dozen different bars on either side of the narrow cobblestone street, the Gown and Gavel is located in a three-storey, century-old building. The main floor dining area is Victorian style, the second floor lounge is completely non-smoking, and the third floor is available for private functions. A full bar sits on the upper deck of the large patio that surrounds the front and the side of the Gown. Another century building next door belonging to the Gown also has a bar and kitchen to serve the busy patio season. A mixed menu includes pizza, nachos and pub fare. Wing specials daily and the take-out hotline is 905-52-WINGS.

❖

The Lionshead
Address: 137 John Street South, Hamilton
Telephone: 905-522-7090
Proprietors: Paul, Chris and Dean
Opened: 1991
Bar: 10 Draft Taps

This small Scottish pub sits in one room with the small sit-down bar at one end and a large window opening out to the street in the summer at the other end, thereby giving it the affectionate nickname of the hole in the wall. This is the only pub I have been to that was recommended by every other publican in town. The atmosphere is friendly and a good laugh is always on hand at the bar. Paul Mason, one of the owners, claims to pour the best pint of Guinness in Hamilton. The menu is pub fare including the popular beer-battered fish and chips. Celtic jam session on Wednesday night and live entertainment Saturdays.

The Pheasant Plucker
Address: 20 Augusta Street, Hamilton
Telephone: 905-529-9000
Proprietor: Malcolm Tosh
Opened: 1998
Bar: 16 Draft Taps

The Pheasant Plucker sits in an 1884 building and still has the original wooden floors. A large brick fireplace in the bar area adds a cozy touch in the colder months. An upstairs dining room is also used for private functions. The pub draws a large soccer contingent and Malcolm, who himself is an Aberdeen fan, always shows the big games. A good selection of single malts available, making the perfect accompaniment for the frequent wild game specials which may include venison, ostrich, wild boar or caribou. The menu features traditional pub fare as well as a daily pasta and a daily catch special. Sunday has two-for-one mussels. Live bands perform every Friday and Saturday evenings.

❖

Slainte

Address: 33 Bowen Street, Hamilton
Telephone: 905-528-8000
Proprietors: Prime Pubs
Opened: 1996
Bar: 15 Draft Taps

This large bar was built in Dublin and shipped over piece by piece along with pub memorabilia for true Irish authenticity. The upstairs has large banquet tables that look like they stepped out of medieval times. The downstairs bar has a natural fireplace with a large stone surround and wooden floorboards. The long sit-down bar stretches down the left side of the room from one end to the other. A traditional pub menu with many popular Irish favourites and in-house specials. Entertainment upstairs Wednesday to Saturday nights, and downstairs occasionally features solo acts on Fridays.

The Tartan Toorie

Address: 587 Concession Street, Hamilton
Telephone: 905-388-0234
Proprietors: Jim and Eileen Kennedy
Opened: 1994
Bar: 9 Draft Taps

Originally a pizza parlour, owner Jim Kennedy completely gutted and renovated the place himself to create a wee bit of Scotland on the mountain. On weekend afternoons you will find many of the regulars sitting at the bar engaged in a "friendly" game of dominoes. A small dart area is off to the side. The menu does contain a selection of pizzas and pasta but the majority of it is Scottish fare, with most of the items homemade. A favourite is the ever-popular square sausage on a roll. Wednesday is an open jam night and once a month the Toorie has a pub night featuring Billy Main and Bouncing Bob; please call for dates.

Ye Olde Squires

Address: 550 Fennel Avenue East, Hamilton
Telephone: 905-388-7770
Proprietor: Graeme Tosh
Opened: 1994
Bar: 17 Draft Taps

A large British pub with a long sit-down bar to the left and a dining area to the right furnished in the traditional style. A large room at the back is available for private parties and adjoining this is a splendid pool room with two tables. A smaller non-smoking dining room with booths is separated from the back room by a large two-sided fireplace. A large-screen TV for all major soccer events. The menu is mainly traditional but includes a mixture of North American and Italian dishes. A large breakfast menu is available Saturdays and Sundays from 10 AM until 2 PM. A popular section of the regular menu is the "chippy" featuring the likes of chips and curry sauce, black pudding and chips, and of course don't forget the fritters. Entertainment every Friday and Saturday night and also Thursdays during the summer.

Lake Simcoe Arms

Address: 21089 Dalton Road, Jackson's Point
Telephone: 905-722-5999/**Web:** http://www.lakesimcoearms.com
Proprietors: Gordon D. Josie
Opened: 2000
Bar: 12 Draft Taps

Situated by the shores of Lake Simcoe, the pub is set in a beautifully designed turn-of-the-century building. Originally built as a hotel, this grand old building has been a licensed premises for over one hundred years. The bar has a large central fireplace in the dining room traditionally furnished with authentic English pub chairs and tables. The interior is one-hundred-year-old reclaimed brick with Tudor ceilings. In the summer the pub hosts many bus groups in conjunction with the local well known Red Barn Theatre. After a night in the Arms one should try one of the many local B & B's or, for that special occasion, the world famous Briars Resort. The menu has a great selection of traditional fare as well as an incredible AAA 18 oz. T-bone steak for the really hearty appetite. An excellent single malt and wine list to compliment your meal.

❖

The Barley Mow

Address: 700 March Road, Kanata
Telephone: 613-599-6098
Proprietors: Gary, Suzanne and Jason
Opened: 1997
Bar: 21 Draft Taps

This bar in Ottawa's high-tech area of Kanata is well equipped to deal with the modern day businessman as it has laptop plug-ins at every table as well as internet access available. Also in the bar are three private snugs, two seat four people while one seats six; this makes for more private meetings and each snug is equipped with a service buzzer. There is a large non-service sit-down bar where people can enjoy a drink while waiting for a table. The bar has a large single malt list and also a good wine selection. There is a large stone fireplace in the dining area. The menu is very varied with many daily specials; wings are on special Monday and Tuesdays 4 PM until close. Entertainment is a mixture of folk, Celtic and light rock every Friday and Saturday night.

The Glen

Address: 462 Hazeldean Road, Kanata
Telephone: 613-836-5622
Proprietor: John McConville
Opened: 1988
Bar: 8 Draft Taps

An authentic Scottish pub and restaurant with tartan wallpaper and plenty of Scottish pictures and memorabilia decorating the walls. The owners and most of the staff hail from the Hamilton area of Scotland and when you close your eyes and listen to them talk you swear you were back in a wee pub just outside Glasgow. Traditional Scottish music plays in the background and the girls all wear tartan waistcoats. The menu is very traditional and contains such favourites as haggis, black pudding and bridies. The pub is also famous for its fish and chips and the haddock can be had battered, breaded or poached.

O'Connor's Irish Pub
Address: 650 Earl Grey Drive, Kanata
Telephone: 613-270-0367
Proprietor: Dave Lispon
Opened: 2001
Bar: 11 Draft Taps

Two large private booths, each with their own entrance, are at the end of the long bar, while another seven booths line the opposite wall. Each booth has its own internet hook-up which proves very popular with the lunch-time business crowd. This bar is like walking into a medieval banquet room, with stone walls and floors, not to mention the occasional suit of armour. The stage has a high stone-wall waterfall which gives an amazing backdrop to the live performers. There is a large pool room at the rear of the bar with three tables. The menu is mainly traditional Irish pub fare with many homemade items. O'Connor's is very much an entertainment bar with Monday being karaoke; Tuesday is reserved for Dave Kalil; Wednesday is open stage night; a d.j. on Thursday; and live bands Fridays and Saturdays.

Royal Oak
Address: 329 March Road, Kanata
Telephone: 613-591-3895
General Manager: Sean Kelly
Opened: 1989
Bar: 17 Draft Taps

Frequented by high tech professionals and residents of Kanata, this is one of the largest Royal Oaks. Three large rooms make up this pub, including a dining area with a central fireplace. Another room can be booked for private parties, with the food tab of the organizer or birthday person picked up by the pub. A large L-shaped bar sits in the centre of the pub and a you will find a pool table in the back room. A pull-down TV screen for all major soccer games. The menu has many traditional dishes, with wings on special Monday, Tuesday and Saturdays. Fish and chips are featured on Fridays. Entertainment every Saturday night and a wonderful Sunday afternoon jazz session from 3 PM to 6 PM.

❖

The Hunt Pub

Address: 12998 Keele Street, King City
Telephone: 905-833-5311
Proprietor: Craig Rose
Opened: 1992
Bar: 10 Draft Taps

Located in the lower level of Hogan's Inn, the Hunt Pub has some of original stone walls dating back to when the place was built in 1851. Leather-backed benches and solid oak tables add to the comfort and cozy atmosphere of this country pub. The small L-shaped bar sits to one side of the charming room and its dark wood fits in perfectly with its surroundings. The inn has fine dining upstairs as well as a casual wine bar with an adjacent covered patio. The wine cellar is well stocked, with over 250 selections to suit every budget and taste. All items on the menu are prepared on the premises. The pub has live entertainment every weekend.

❖

Kingston Brewing Company

Address: 34 Clarence Street, Kingston
Telephone: 613-542-4978
Brewmaster: Roger Eccleston
Opened: 1986
Bar: 12 Draft Taps

Ask nicely and Roger the brewmaster will give you a guided tour of the brewing process. The bar features many ales and lagers brewed on the premises. Many are seasonal and subject to availability, however Dragon's Breath Real Ale, which is the most popular, can be had all year round. Micro guest beers are on tap and are frequently rotated along with cask-conditioned ales. A selection of over 100 single malts is available and the bar is also the headquarters of the local An Quaich society. Upstairs has a small brewery artifacts museum, with many of the items being found by customers diving in nearby waters. The pub has probably the largest collection of bar towels in Canada and all are proudly displayed on the walls. The menu is varied and includes a smokehouse section, with all the food smoked on the premises. Another part of the menu features the "High Roller Special," which is a bottle of Dom Perignon and a double order of wings.

The Pilot House

Address: 265 King Street East, Kingston
Telephone: 613-542-0222
Proprietor: Ron Easteal
Opened: 1981
Bar: 14 Draft Taps

Well known for its fish and chips, the small bar is always busy with patrons having a brew while waiting for their meal. The dining area is small and most times it is hard to get a table. The menu is similar to many British seaside town restaurants and Ron spent a few years in Cornwall, where fishing and seafood are a way of life. A patio on the sidestreet is known as the deck and is popular with tourists and locals alike. The restaurant does have dartboards but most of the time the place is too busy for anyone to play.

❖

Tir nan Og

Address: 200 Ontario Street, Kingston
Telephone: 613-544-7474
General Manager: Jeff Girling
Opened: 1996
Bar: 28 Draft Taps

A large bar with so many rooms that it takes a minute or two to get orientated. There is a cigar bar called Monte's and on the lower level a bar called the Old Speckle. The main bar has an area with a grand stone fireplace in a section bordered by wrought iron and set on a stone floor. The rest of the bar has wooden floors to capture the authenticity of bygone days. It is not unusual to see people walking through this pub as if they were touring a museum. The menu is traditional pub fare and a lot more with a late selection available from 10 PM until 2 AM. Live bands on Friday and Saturday nights with jazz every Friday in Monte's.

The Toucan and Kirkpatrick's

Address: 76 Princess Street, Kingston
Telephone: 613-544-1966/**Web:** http://www.thetoucan.ca
Proprietors: Art Robinson and Bruce Clark
Opened: 1986
Bar: 20 Draft Taps

This well-known Kingston pub is actually two in one, with the lower level being the Toucan and the upper Kirkpatrick's. Well known by soccer and rugby fans alike, the bar shows all major games and many a time it's standing room only. Owner Art Robinson played professional soccer for Middlesborough in the late 50s, while partner Bud Gormley was the man behind the drive to bring a part of the 1976 Olympics to Kingston, in which he succeeded. The menu has a large traditional section with many homemade pies, a favourite being the curried beef with a light puff pastry topping. Sunday, Monday and Tuesday wings are on special from two in the afternoon. The wings are said to be the best in Kingston. Every Monday entertainment by the Blue Monday Blues Band.

Molly Bloom's

Address: 10 Manitou Drive. Kitchener
Telephone: 519-894-4445
Proprietors: Ted Connelly and Brian Watson
Opened: 2000
Bar: 16 Draft Taps

The bar has timber ceilings, reclaimed brick walls and a large dining area with a central dance floor. The bar area has a separate darts section and a big screen television. Located in a large plaza with plenty of parking. The menu is very varied with the following evening specials: Tuesday — Wings; Wednesday — Chicken and ribs; Thursday — Schnitzel. Open jam session every Wednesday and live music on Friday and Saturday nights, where it is not unusual to see Annie jump from behind the bar to go up and give you a wee Scottish song.

Lindsay

Coach and Horses

Address: 16 York Street South, Lindsay
Proprietor: David Smith
Opened: 1988
Bar: 5 Draft Taps

A popular student hang-out from September to April and the home of the best darts team in Lindsay, this pub shows all major sporting events, especially soccer. A pool table and a table-top football game sit at one end of the bar and a juke box is continually in use at the other end. The menu is a mix of pub fare and finger foods, with excellent meat pies especially the steak and kidney. Tuesday is special draft night and entertainment is periodical; please call for details.

The Winchester Arms

Address: 47 William Street North, Lindsay
Telephone: 705-878-4312
Manager: Donna
Opened: 1995
Bar: 11 Draft Taps

A large bookcase partition runs down the centre of the bar, separating the bar area from the dining room. A small room with a capacity for 24 can be booked for luncheons, office parties, etc. The pub has a total of four dartboards and a pool table. A separate lunch menu is available, while the main menu is a mixture of traditional pub fare including Melton mowbry pie, and sandwiches. A favourite item is the Robin Hood pie, which is a delicious homemade steak and kidney pie. For an extra 99¢ you can complement your meal with a fresh-baked loaf. Entertainment periodical; please call for details.

London

Dick O'Dows

Address: 483 Richmond Street, London
Telephone: 519-672-5554
Proprietors: Jason Fitzmorris and David Massarella
Opened: 2000
Bar: 8 Draft Taps

Large barn floorboards give the interior of this pub an authentic aged look. The upper level has numerous booths and a dartboard area. A large gas fireplace sits central in the lower bar area and in the summer the most popular table is the one by the open window looking out onto the street. The bar stocks a good selection of single malts and Irish whiskies. Traditional pub fare with a good selection of curries and appetizers. Entertainment Fridays and Saturdays during the summer and Tuesdays, Thursdays, Fridays and Saturdays when the students are back in university.

❖

Liam Brannigan's

Address: 355 Wellington Street, Unit 159, London
Telephone: 519-434-7888
Proprietor: Liam Brannigan
Opened: 2000
Bar: 8 Draft Taps

A traditional Irish pub with plenty of spacious booths and a cozy snug at the end of the bar. A good selection of single malts and fine Irish whiskies with the bar hosting occasional tastings. A large striking glass mirror behind the bar bears the pub's name. Owner Liam is an accomplished chef and his menu is traditionally Irish with some very traditional side dishes including champ, which is mashed potatoes with garlic and scallions. An in-house favourite are curry sticks and are a closely guarded secret recipe. Every Wednesday Lisa Reilly hosts an open stage session and weekend entertainment is live Celtic music.

The Elephant and Castle
Address: 333-335 Wellington Street, London
Telephone: 519-434-4554
General Manager: Jack Oatman
Opened: 1983
Bar: 11 Draft Taps
Situated in London's large Galleria Mall, if you arrange to meet anyone at this pub make sure you tell them what part, as this pub is multi-leveled and has rooms and indoor patios at every turn. Many parts of the pub open onto the indoor mall, including a couple of small patios that offer a welcome break from shopping. Pool tables are in a sunken area with natural lighting provided by the large sky lights of the mall 60 feet above. A separate room named the Canterbury can be booked free of charge for meetings and private functions. The menu is a large mix of traditional and North American and appetizers are on special Monday to Friday from 4 PM to 6 PM. Entertainment on Thursday, Friday and Saturday nights.

Molly Bloom's
Address: 700 Richmond Street, London
Telephone: 519-675-1212
Proprietors: Mike O'Brien
Opened: 1999
Bar: 18 Draft Taps
A few steps down from street level on the ground floor of the Selby building, this pub's décor is a warm blend of brick and wood. The Selby is a high-rise office tower and many of its workers can be found in the Molly at cocktail hour. The pub has many large sections, which are great for sports teams, and a small snug at the opposite end of the bar. A large patio seats over one hundred and is the perfect place for train spotting as it borders a very busy railway line. The menu is a good mix of traditional fare and a selection of sandwiches and wraps. Monday and Tuesday are wing nights and the pub has entertainment seven nights a week.

The Poacher's Arms

Address: 171 Queens Avenue, London
Telephone: 519-432-7888
Proprietors: Danny and Irene
Opened: 1984
Bar: 15 Draft Taps

The Poacher is very popular with fans of the English national soccer team whenever there is a game being shown on their two large screens. The pub is also the base for the London Glasgow Rangers supporters club. A large bar area has two pool tables while there is a separate dart room with several tables perfect for tournament and team play. A separate dining room has numerous booths and a large stone fireplace at one end. The menu is varied and has a large pizza selection as well as traditional homemade fare. Entertainment every Friday and Saturday night.

The Scots Corner

Address: 268 Dundas Street, London
Telephone: 519-667-2277
Proprietor: Billy Thomson
Opened: 1998
Bar: 28 Draft Taps

The sit-down bar serves both the pub side and the lounge and it is in the lounge that you will find the soccer lads when the games are being shown. In the pub side there is a stand-up snug along with a pool table and two large screens for all major soccer games including Scottish premier. Tables by a large corner fireplace prove to be a popular spot in the colder months. The menu is traditional pub fare with a favourite choice being the large Scottish breakfast. Wings are on special everyday. Entertainment seven nights a week, with an open stage with Vinnie on Thursdays.

❖

Waltzing Weasel

Address: 1326 Adelaide Street North, London
Telephone: 519-663-9194/**Web:** http://www.waltzingweasel.com
Proprietor: Mike McCoubrey
Opened: 1998
Bar: 20 Draft Taps

Standing in an impressive heritage building on the corner of
Adelaide and Windermere, this pub is neighbour to a 36-hole
mini golf course and combined they make a great way to spend
the afternoon. A reclaimed brick interior is in keeping with the
charm of this century-old building. An upstairs room is available
for private functions and is also used as an overflow due to busy
dinner periods. A traditional pub fare menu with a good selection
of finger foods. Monday nights are wing specials and a brunch
menu is available on Sundays.

Wits End Pub

Address: 235 North Centre Road, London
Telephone: 519-850-9487/**Web:** http://www.witsendpub.com
Proprietor: Deb O'Brien
Opened: 1999
Bar: 18 Draft Taps

Named restaurant of the year by the Ontario Restaurant, Hotel and Motel Association for the London area for the year 2001, this pub's owner, Deb O'Brien, goes all out to promote and make her pub what it is, including advertising on local radio and splashing the bar's name all over a London transit bus. The bar is two level with the top section being the bar area and the lower for dining and entertainment. The dining area has booths with unique fish lights, which keep the kids occupied and let you enjoy your meal in peace. Three satellite dishes make sure you don't miss any sporting events on the giant screen. The menu is large and very varied with a large pasta and Californian salads selection. The kitchen is open concept where you can watch your meals being cooked on the large grill. Sundays and Wednesdays are all-you-can-eat wing night and Mondays between 5 PM and 9 PM are all-you-can-eat ribs. Karaoke Tuesday and Thursday and live music at the weekends.

The Duchess of Markham

Address: 53 Main Street North, Markham
Telephone: 905-294-3181
Proprietor: Mike Thompson
Opened: 1980
Bar: 16 Draft Taps

A beautiful little pub in the heritage part of Markham's old Main Street, with traditional Tudor styling and red window frames making it picture perfect. The sit-down bar is separated from the dining area by a waist-high wooden partition, which is needed for when you lean back to let people pass by the busy bar area. The small dining area has a corner fireplace that adds to the traditional décor of the room. A large portion of the clientele are from the British Isles and most have been regulars from day one. Upstairs handles the overspill on busy nights and the room can also be booked for private parties. The large patio features entertainment with Midtown every Sunday afternoon, weather permitting, and it has its own full-service cabana bar. The menu is mostly traditional with many excellent daily specials. The well-known Scottish entertainer Syd Simkins plays every Friday night and the aforementioned Midtown every Wednesday.

❖

Fox and Fiddle

Address: 144 Main Street North, Markham
Telephone: 905-294-4600
General Manager: Cynthia Shaw
Opened: 2000
Bar: 16 Draft Taps

This pub is situated in the Wilson House, a heritage building named after a doctor who practiced there at the turn of the century. The main floor is made up of cozy sections each in their own unique area, including the small sit-down bar which is tucked away into a corner. Across from the bar is the solarium, a very popular spot especially when the windows are open and a gentle breeze is flowing through the bar. The menu is varied and includes traditional pub dishes with a good selection of sandwiches and wraps. Prime rib dinner with Yorkshire pudding is the excellent Saturday special. A good selection of single malts and wine are also available. Upstairs has entertainment every Thursday, Friday and Saturday nights.

❖

Markham

King Edward's Arms
Address: 8505 Warden Avenue, Markham
Telephone: 905-305-9525
Proprietor: Ted D. Mitroff
Opened: 1997
Bar: 17 Draft Taps
Being located in a large plaza means plenty of parking for this very cozy traditional English-style pub with a small sit-down bar to the left as you go in and an upper dining area to the right. The walls are covered in prints of old English pubs and this adds to the authentic feel of the place. Finding a table at lunch and dinner hours can be difficult as the traditional homemade fare and the many daily specials are proving to be very popular; however a seat at the bar with the friendly regulars and staff make the wait worthwhile. A good selection of single malts to be had.

Owl and Firkin
Address: 7181 Woodbine Avenue, Markham
Telephone: 905-513-6611
Proprietor: Malcolm Martin
Opened: 1998
Bar: 16 Draft Taps
Located around the corner from IBM, the Owl does a roaring lunchtime trade especially in the summer, when the large patio is always busy. The square sit-down bar is in the centre of the pub and the bar area has an elevated section with bench seating and tables. The dining area is down to the left as you enter and features a row of booths. The Owl has two pool tables, two dartboards, two Golden Tees and a juke box as well as a bar top video game. A large menu with many lunch and dinner specials. Every night has ribs and wings on special.

The Sheltie Pub
Address: 6061 Highway 7 East, Markham
Telephone: 905-471-2469
Proprietor: Bob Burkitt
Opened: 1996
Bar: 16 Draft Taps

An open-concept pub with the sit-down bar bordering the far wall as you enter the main dining area with its traditional carpeting and comfortable seating. A large three-sided glass fireplace sits in the centre of the room and adds warmth to the whole pub. The menu is a mix of traditional and North American fare with many daily specials. A pub tradition for four years, Thursday nights are always busy when Jim McHarg's Jazzmen are playing. Friday has karaoke, which features cash prizes, and a live band entertains on Saturdays.

Merrickville

The Goose and Gridiron
Address: 317 St. Lawrence Street, Merrickville
Telephone: 613-269-2094
Proprietors: Tracy and Rob Sine
Opened: 199
Bar: 10 Draft Taps

Known as the Jewel of the Rideau, historical Merrickville is where you will find this traditional country inn with the red phone box outside. Named after a pub in London where on June 24, 1717, the grand lodge of freemasonry in England was founded, to which all of the grand lodges trace their charters. Two separate dining sections and a banquet room, which is available for private parties, along with the copper-topped bar make up the main floor of this circa-1856 building. Included in the draft selection is the in-house Goose brown ale, a local favourite. The menu is mostly home-cooked pub fare and features the massive English mixed grill for the hearty appetite. Monday and Thursday are wing nights. Entertainment on Thursday, Friday and Saturday evenings.

❖

The Dickens

Address: 189 Mill Street, Milton
Telephone: 905-878-9040
Proprietor: Stan Mishaud
Opened: 1980
Bar: 12 Draft Taps

The interior of this traditional English pub is like stepping into a Victorian parlour; one expects to see Dickens himself working on his latest book. This busy neighbourhood pub has been catering to British exiles for over 20 years and many of them have been coming here from opening day. The patio has brick pillars that support wooden cross beams from which drape beautiful hanging baskets in constant bloom. Upstairs can be used for private functions or hosting ball teams after tournaments. The menu is very traditional, with a fish and chip special on Monday, ribs on Thursday and the very popular prime rib dinner featured Friday to Sunday from 5 PM to 10 PM. Karaoke every Saturday evening.

The Ivy Arms

Address: 201 Main Street, Milton
Telephone: 905-876-4899
Proprietors: Harry Brown, Steve Brown and Ken Phillips
Opened: 2000
Bar: 13 Draft Taps

Harry and Steve Brown between them have custom built over two hundred pubs and even now while owning their own bar their skills are still in high demand. The bar is on two levels with the downstairs open all winter and available for private functions in the summer. May to October the busy Main street is blocked off on Saturdays for Milton's farmers' market with the bar opening at 9 AM to serve breakfast. The menu features traditional fare and a good selection of pasta. Every Friday, Saturday and Sunday in the warmer months an outdoor barbecue is available on the patio. Entertainment every second Saturday evening.

The Belfast Lounge

Address: 5165 Dixie Road, Mississauga
Telephone: 905-212-9048/**Web:** http://www.belfastlounge.com
Proprietors: Colin and Victor McCullough
Opened: 1999
Bar: 14 Draft Taps

This upscale restaurant and pub has an abundance of Beaujolais-stained oak on the walls, bar, tables and chairs, giving the pub a rich Victorian look. The long green velvet–upholstered benches are very comfortable, or one can cozy up in one of the two private booths, which can accommodate up to 12 people. The lounge has large black leather chairs, a handsome fireplace and stained glass accents. The walls are adorned with oil paintings of Irish countryside and historical Belfast sites. The menu offers a variety of dishes, with traditional Irish fare as well as pastas, pizzas and entrees including steaks and curried chicken. The bar has an excellent selection of Irish beers, great whiskies and fine wines.

The Brogue Pub

Address: 136 Lakeshore Road East, Port Credit, Mississauga
Telephone: 905-278-8444
Proprietor: Tommy Donnelly
Opened: 2000
Bar: 14 Draft Taps

This new addition to picturesque Port Credit has a bar to the left when you walk in and a separate dining room to the right. The bar has a good selection of Scotch and Irish whiskys and its menu is traditional pub fare with an Irish flair. The dining room is elegantly furnished, complete with a beautiful stone fireplace. The menu here is quite extensive and cosmopolitan with an excellent wine list. An annual lobster and seafood festival runs while the catch is good throughout the summer. Entertainment Thursdays and Saturdays, with Celtic bands playing on the Thursday.

❖

Coopers Pub

Address: 780 Burnhamthorpe Road West, Unit 5, Mississauga
Telephone: 905-275-3245
Proprietor: Damian McKerr
Opened: 1991
Bar: 23 Draft Taps

The pub has many unique Irish photographs and prints adorning the walls and a large gas fire with a reclaimed brick surround adds character and warmth to the centre of the room. It's easy to join in the conversation at the large oval sit-down bar at the far end of the pub. There is a dart room at the back allowing players to practice in peace. A large pull-down TV screen is regularly in use during major sporting events. The large menu is a traditional/North American mix with wing specials on Monday and Tuesday evenings, the pub night sees burgers, nachos, wings and draft specials on Wednesdays. Live bands Thursday, Friday and Saturday nights.

The Devil's Harp

Address: 1201 Britannia Road West, Mississauga
Telephone: 905-816-1776
Proprietor: Quinn Harper
Opened: 2000
Bar: 20 Draft Taps

High ceilings and Tudor styling with many large beams give the interior the look of an old rustic English farmhouse. A large open-concept bar with a small alcove to the right as you enter contains dartboards and window seating. There are a couple of booths over by the big-screen TV which shows a double feature on Sunday "movie" nights starting at 7 PM. The menu is varied with many pub favourites and the following evening specials: Monday — Two-for-one wings; Tuesday — Fish and chips; Wednesday — Full rack of ribs; Thursday and Saturday: Two-for-one pasta; Friday — Prime rib special. Karaoke on Thursday night and live bands on Friday.

Docherty's
Address: 4230 Sherwoodtowne Boulevard, Mississauga
Telephone: 905-897-0900
Proprietor: Jim Gentle
Opened: 1997
Bar: 12 Draft Taps

This cozy pub has a narrow traditional bar area with a small games room that includes a pool table and dartboards. A separate bistro-style dining room is off to the side. The menu includes traditional fare as well as a selection of pizza, sandwiches and wraps. Monday night has wings on special and Thursday is ladies' night with complimentary appetizers. Entertainment is periodical and usually a theme night featuring dinner and a show. Previous evenings have seen Elvis and crooner nights; call for details.

Drake and Firkin
Address: 6982 Financial Drive, Unit B101, Mississauga
Telephone: 905-567-9173
Proprietors: Sandi and Kristy
Opened: 2001
Bar: 16 Draft Taps

The newest Firkin is a traditional English neighbourhood family pub restaurant concept with the philosophy, "A beer you can get anywhere, but good food is hard to come by." The menu choices are broad, ranging from traditional English fare to AAA-grade Canadian beef steaks to vegetarian dishes. The pub also has exceptional daily specials including a pie, catch and pasta of the day. Located in a large business area, the Drake is a welcome addition for the many local offices at lunch and dinner hours. A large patio with seating for 90 provides the perfect setting for outdoor meals. The pub also features two pool tables, a dartboard and the NTN trivia game.

The Duke of Marlborough
Address: 680 Silver Creek Boulevard, Mississauga
Telephone: 905-275-9301
Proprietor: Guerrino Staropoli
Opened: 1981
Bar: 8 Draft Taps

This quaint little pub is located in the lower level of Mississauga's oldest surviving house. The house is called Cherry Hill and was built in 1822; a fine dining restaurant bearing the same name sits above the pub. The pub has large wooden beams and a natural brick surround fireplace sitting on a flagstone floor. The building was moved a few hundred yards to its present location in 1973 where it was restored to its original splendour. The menu is traditional with many daily specials including the popular build-your-own omelette. Well known for its soccer coverage, the Duke shows many games on its large screen. In May the pub is surrounded by blossoming cherry trees.

Failte
Address: 201 City Centre Drive, Mississauga
Telephone: 905-276-2212
Proprietor: Damian McKerr
Opened: 1998
Bar: 12 Draft Taps

Designed in Dublin and with authentic Irish memorabilia throughout, this pub is truly impressive. Failte is divided into many parts depicting the many faces of Ireland: there is the old cottage with its stone walls and rustic look, the chemist's bar, and also a Victorian parlour complete with replica Victorian furniture. A small authentic village grocery store sits in its own little nook and the entertainment area is the medieval room. The menu features many traditional Irish dishes and exceptional daily specials. Celtic music on Thursdays and live bands Friday and Saturday nights. A multi-leveled spacious patio brings you back to Canada.

Fox and Fiddle

Address: 285 Enfield Place, Mississauga
Telephone: 905-566-1355
General Manager: Bill Ganas
Opened: 1989
Bar: 20 Draft Taps

A long stand-up bar runs parallel to the sit-down bar making for a very popular busy spot in this pub, voted the best in Mississauga last year by Toronto Sun readers. A large brick surround fireplace stands grandly in the centre of the dining area, which contains plenty of booths for a more intimate meal. Another separate dining area is designated non-smoking. The menu has a good mixture of traditional and North American fare with a daily curry special and a Tuesday wing night. Monday nights feature the popular Tom Barlow and live bands appear every Thursday, Friday and Saturday.

Fox and Fiddle

Address: 3055 Dundas Street, Mississauga
Telephone: 905-607-4810
General Manager: Jany Skentzos-Maraby
Opened: 1990
Bar: 24 Draft Taps

A games room containing dartboards and video games is off to the right as you enter this large Mississauga pub while the long L-shaped bar is straight ahead. Two pool tables are at the opposite end of the room with a large dining area in between. A dining lounge aptly named the Library with a central fireplace and book-shelves makes up another section. The large patio is complete with its own bar which is in use during theme nights and parties. A large mixed menu with half-price appetizers daily from 4 PM to 6 PM, wings are on special Thursday and Friday nights after 10 PM, Wednesday is ladies' night and includes half-price fajitas. There's aD.J. on Wednesday, Thursday and Saturday nights, while Thursday is an open jam night with a bar prize for all participants.

❖

Hare and Firkin

Address: 2800 Skymark Avenue, Unit 28, Mississauga
Telephone: 905-624-4273
Proprietor: Andrea Casale
Opened: 199
Bar: 16 Draft Taps

Walk through the front doors and the first thing to greet you is a large three-sided fireplace. The pub is surrounded by many windows that allow for plenty of natural light. There is a non-smoking dining area while the two-level bar and a small sitting section accommodate smokers. The pub has many booths and glass partitions along with a tin ceiling creating an atmosphere that is rather intimate and comfortable. A mixed menu including many daily specials with the wings and appetizers on special Monday and Tuesday nights. The Hare has two pool tables and a dart area. Entertainment normally from January until April, please call for details.

The Harp

Address: 55 Lakeshore Road East, Mississauga
Telephone: 905-274-3277
Proprietor: Maureen O'Neill-Pikul
Opened: 198
Bar: 18 Draft Taps

One of the first Irish pubs in Mississauga and still one of its favourites; the Harp was voted the best pub by the Mississauga News readers for the year 2001. Large-screen TVs for all sporting events, especially the N.F.L. on Sundays. The menu is a varied mix ranging from traditional to international cuisine. including Indian selections such as the curry of the day. Nightly specials are as follows: Monday — All you can eat spaghetti; Tuesday — All you can eat mussels; Thursday — All you can eat ribs. Monday and Tuesday are also wing nights. Breakfast specials Saturday and Sundays. Celtic bands every Wednesday, jazz every Thursday, live bands every Friday and Saturday and house band, the Meteors, every Sunday night.

Lion and Leprechaun

Address: 1900 Dundas Street West, Mississauga
Telephone: 905-855-3913
Proprietor: Pat Moore
Opened: 1999
Bar: 17 Draft Taps

A large three-level patio wraps around the pub giving access to all-day sun, or shade if you prefer. The pub has many sections including larger areas perfect for giving sports teams their own space, an upstairs room with pool tables and dartboards is available for functions. A large mixed menu with traditional dishes and an East Indian selection. Evening specials are as follows: Monday — Pizza; Tuesday — Wings; Wednesday — Pasta; Thursday — Curry; Friday — N.Y. strip loin. Saturday and Sunday the bar features a big breakfast from 11 AM until 3 PM. Entertainment on Thursday nights.

Mad Dogs and Englishmen

Address: 2157 Royal Windsor Drive, Mississauga
Telephone: 905-855-0217
Proprietor: Joanne Ardill
Opened: 2000
Bar: 19 Draft Taps

Situated in a large plaza with plenty of parking, the Mad Dog is a traditional English-style bar with an open concept and lots of booths around the perimeter. A pool table is at the far end of the pub and dartboards are just as you walk in. The menu is varied with a good selection of traditional and North American fare and excellent daily specials. A big screen for the local soccer boys; the pub shows all the major games. Entertainment on Monday nights is by the popular Paul Stephens and live bands are featured every Friday.

The Mad Hatter

Address: 4646 Heritage Hill Boulevard, Mississauga
Telephone: 905-501-9048
Proprietor: Charlie
Opened: 1996
Bar: 16 Draft Taps

The pub is housed in a rustic red brick heritage building which was built in the 1850s and the adjoining plaza was allowed to go ahead only if they matched this lovely old house, which they did perfectly. The bar has traditional English décor from the thick carpeting to the upholstered bench seating. A room at the far end has a small stand-up bar and a big-screen TV; another large pull-down screen is at the other end, which allows patrons to view major sports from any angle. A traditional-fare menu with wings on special everyday after 4 PM. Saturday and Sunday the Hatter serves brunch from 11 AM until 2 PM.

The Rampant and Rose

Address: 3200 Erin Mills Road, Unit 9, Mississauga
Telephone: 905-608-9603
Proprietors: Barry Miller and Dwight Beaton
Opened: 2001
Bar: 20 Draft Taps

A large wooden bookcase at one end of this pub complements the brick interior, while long benches make perfect seating for large groups or teams. A small patio is surrounded by shrubs, which give a nice garden feel to outdoor lunches. A large room round the side has dartboards, and a big-screen TV is at the door as you walk in. The menu mixes traditional and North American fare with wing specials on Monday nights and two-for-one pasta on Tuesday. An 8-oz. sirloin is the dish of choice on Fridays and an all-day breakfast is available at the weekend. Live bands perform every Thursday.

Rooster and Firkin

Address: 723 Central Parkway West. Mississauga
Telephone: 905-275-6900
Proprietor: Kevin Rochwerg
Opened: 200
Bar: 16 Draft Taps

The Rooster is located on the northeast corner of Mavis Road and Central Parkway West. The bar consists of three main sections including a raised dining area to the left. A games area is around the back and consists of two pool tables, darts and a Golden Tee golf game. The interior is flanked on three sides by large windows, which make for a very bright, airy establishment. The full menu contains many traditional dishes and delightful daily specials. Monday and Tuesday are wing nights while Saturday features a Corona beer and large nacho special. Wednesday come and join in the casino/black jack evening. Entertainment weekly features karaoke and live music; please call for dates and times.

The Winchester Arms

Address: 1852 Lakeshore Road West, Mississauga
Telephone: 905-855-7489
Proprietors: Kary and Gary Cupples
Opened: 1989
Bar: 13 Draft Taps

As you enter the Winchester, the sit-down bar is to your left and the main dining area straight ahead; the pub is a mixture of tables and bench seating. A room downstairs contains a pool table and dartboards. The pub is situated in a strip plaza with plenty of parking in the evenings. The menu is a good mix of traditional and North American, with lunch and dinner specials. The following are the permanent specials: Monday — Wings, Tuesday — Twoonie Tuesday featuring food and drink specials; Wednesday — Curry night; Thursday — Two-for-one lunches; Friday — Fish and chips. Sunday has a draft and wing special to coincide with the NFL on the big screen. A game of euchre is available on Monday nights, live entertainment every Thursday, while Friday is karaoke night. Saturday evenings are various pub nights.

Peter Cellars Pub

Address: RR#1, Mono Centre
Telephone: 519-941-5109
Proprietor: Carol Hall
Opened: 1987
Bar: 2 Draft Taps

Located in the basement of the Mono Cliffs Inn, this quaint little pub has bench seating around the walls and a small snug/booth that seats two. There is a wood-burning stove in the corner and the walls are decorated with photographs of the late great Peter Sellers. The Mono Cliffs Inn is located directly across from Mono Cliffs Provincial Park, which features marvelous scenery and many trails. The Inn has fine dining on the main level, and the McLaren Room, available for private functions. The pub has a great selection of over 40 single malts to choose from and an equally good wine list. The wine cellar in the room next to the pub seats eight and is perfect for small, intimate special occasions. The menu is upscale but at pub prices with exceptional daily specials. Entertainment every Friday evening. The pub is only open Fridays, Saturdays and Sundays and holiday Mondays.

❖

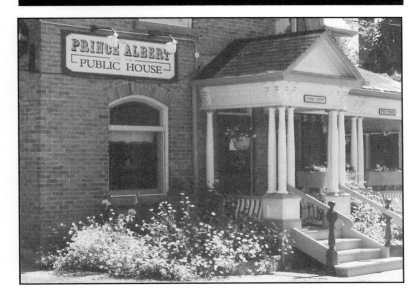

The Prince Albert

Address: 69 Main Street, Mount Albert
Telephone: 905-473-1629
Publican: Ian Bowie
Opened: 1998
Bar: 11 Draft Taps

The Prince Albert is located in the small town of Mount Albert which is on Highway 48, a few miles north of Newmarket. The pub stands in the Lloyd house built in 1906 and locally known as "the bat house" but you will have to ask Ian the story behind that. A small bar area is downstairs with another room housing a dining area, while upstairs has a dart room and pool tables. This old manse has a small veranda out front and while having a beer out there you feel like you are visiting an old friend. The bar has a good selection of single malts and hosts frequent Scotch nosings; please call for details. The menu is a good selection of pub fare with special deals on "leftover Mondays." A roast beef dinner is the special on weekends and Sunday also has a breakfast buffet.

❖

The Crow's Nest

Address: 115 Prospect Street, Newmarket
Telephone: 905-953-8776
General Manager: Brent Riopelle
Opened: 1998
Bar: 20 Draft Taps

Low lighting along with rich carpeting and traditional wallpaper gives this pub a warm, comfortable atmosphere. The dining area is tastefully decorated with a mix of Scottish prints and antique memorabilia. A central fireplace adds to the relaxed and cozy ambience. The bar area is to one side and Scottish theme room is available upstairs for private parties. The Crow's Nest prides itself on the quality of its menu and the word has spread, with lunch and dinner hours very busy. The menu features a great variety of dishes, including a traditional pub fare section. The halibut and chips are one of the more popular choices along with the following daily specials: Monday — Half-price wings; Tuesday — Pasta of the day; Wednesday and Thursday — a delicious rib dinner; Saturday and Sunday between 11 AM and 3 PM a brunch menu is available. During golfing season, golfers show their same-day green fee and receive a free pound of wings with any pint of beer purchased. The pub puts on frequent Scotch nosing nights and over 30 brands are available at the bar.

❖

Fox and Fiddle

Address: 446 Davis Drive, Newmarket
Telephone: 905-836-6982
General Manager: Sherri Groves.
Opened: 2001
Bar: 20 Draft Taps

A long sit-down bar with a copper tone leaf-imprinted countertop sits central in this latest addition to the Fox and Fiddle family. Two pool tables and golf games are off to the left. Two dining areas and a dance floor make up the rest of the pub. Customers will never miss any action, as the bar has 13 televisions including a large pull-down screen. An upstairs banquet room is available for hire and has a capacity for over 200. The menu is a good mix of traditional and North American fare with the following evening specials: Monday — Wings and things; Tuesday — Two can dine for $14.99; Wednesday — Fajitas and margarita night; Sundays are five buck special days. A disc jockey is featured on Thursday, Friday and Saturday nights, Tuesday is jam night and karaoke is on Wednesday. The Thursday night session is also ladies night with martini specials. A pub with something for everyone.

The Grey Goat

Address: 74 Main Street South, Newmarket
Telephone: 905-895-7902
Proprietors: Joel and Jan Phillips
Opened: 1982
Bar: 12 Draft Taps

The Goat sits on a slight incline in a 135-year-old building and the large patio deck offers a grand view of Main Street below. The small pub downstairs with its wooden floors has the look and feel of an authentic country pub. Upstairs is a charming lounge with warm décor and a natural stone fireplace; this room can be booked for private parties and has its own full-service bar. The menu features traditional pub fare with many daily specials. Wings are on special Wednesday nights. A Tuesday night jam session is fast becoming the place to be, with many talented musicians getting up to play, including the Goat's very own Randy. Saturday features live music.

❖

The Hound and Heather
Address: 465 Davis Drive, Newmarket
Telephone: 905-836-4069
Proprietor: Graham
Opened: 1992
Bar: 13 Draft Taps

Located on the ground floor of the magnificent stone and marble Tannery Mall, this pub features granite walls and a 30-foot sit-down bar. Right next to the Go train station, it's the perfect place to relax after the commute from the city. A pool table and big-screen TV are on the upper dining level, while the opposite section contains dartboards and a large dance floor. The menu is a mix of traditional and North American fare and features the following evening specials: Tuesday — Wings; Wednesday — Steak; Thursday — Jug and Nachos; Friday — Fish and chips; Saturday — prime rib dinner. For entertainment the Hound has the best rock bands north of Toronto, for which there is a small cover charge. Thursday night is ladies' night and features the best in new music by the house disc jockey.

Lion and Firkin
Address: 1091 Gorham Street, Newmarket
Telephone: 905-853-0050
Proprietor: Gary
Opened: 1997
Bar: 16 Draft Taps

With a distinctive English pub flavour the bar section of the Lion has a darts area and a few stand-up tables, while the pool table sits in a sunken section with two-storey-high glass windows allowing for plenty of natural light. The restaurant side with a capacity in excess of one hundred is very traditional in décor and features many booths. A busy place at lunch and cocktail hours, the Lion offers many excellent daily food specials. The wings are on special every Saturday, Sunday and Monday evening. NTN trivia is available at the bar. Live entertainment every Thursday and Sunday features karaoke.

The Mad Hatter
Address: 17725 Yonge Street, Newmarket
Telephone: 905-853-4775
Proprietors: Bill and Lorne
Opened: 1999
Bar: 16 Draft Taps

A large open-concept, with the sit-down bar a few steps up from the main dining area, the Hatter is a British-style pub with traditional décor and carpeting. The non-smoking dining area features a cozy corner fireplace and bench seating. The pub shows all major soccer events on the big screen, including English F.A. Cup games. The menu is traditional pub fare plus colonial choices with Monday and Tuesday being wing night and Thursday through Sunday the house specialty, delicious prime rib dinners. Every Saturday features the best in local entertainment ranging from traditional to modern. All-day entertainment and food specials on the big St.Patrick's Day party.

The Angel Inn

Address: 224 Regent Street, Niagara-on-the-Lake
Telephone: 905-468-3411
Proprietors: Peter and Diane Ling
Opened: Early 1800s
Bar: 20 Draft Taps

Burned down in the War of 1812 and rebuilt around 1818, the Angel Inn has been serving travelers and locals alike for over 200 years. The small basement pub has flaming fireplaces, hand-hewn beams and worn, wide pine floor boards. A hearty menu, including the favourite steak, Guinness and oyster pie, which Peter first tasted in Dublin. The main dining room has a large oil painting of King John reluctantly putting his seal on the Magna Carta; on another wall is a one-third carving of The Mermaid of Caen, copied by Geoff Stead from a famous wood carving in the abbey of Caen, Normandy. The Inn stocks a large selection of local wines and is well known for its hospitality. But it is probably best known for its resident ghost, Captain Colin Swayze, a Canadian militia officer who was killed in the cellar during the U.S. invasion of Niagara in 1813. Legend has it that he went to the cellar during a lull in the fighting to visit a barmaid or to rescue some army-issue rum stored there. His death was at the hands of American soldiers searching the property. A Union Jack flies over the front door of the Inn today; they say that this keeps the ghost in the cellar. For the brave soul who spends a night at the Inn, a certificate is presented next day stating you "survived" the night. The Angel is a must-see for visitors to the picturesque Niagara-on-the-Lake area. Entertainment every Friday and Saturday night.

❖

The Bull and Quench
Address: 603 McIntyre East, North Bay
Telephone: 705-840-2855
Proprietors: Deb and Rich
Opened: 1996
Bar: 12 Draft Taps

The pub was created and designed after owners Deb and Rich experienced first hand the friendliness of the British local. Relax in the downstairs pub with its traditional wallpaper décor and casual atmosphere and experience the friendly personal attention you will receive from your hosts. The upstairs has a pool table and shuffleboard and also a large-screen TV for the sports fan; this room is also available for special occasions. The menu has a large selection of traditional fare as well as Canadian pub favourites. The beer-battered fish and chips seem to be the most popular choice and for the really big appetite there is the Bully burger, which weighs in at a whopping 16 oz., or for the really, really big appetite double it up to the 32-oz. Matador. Entertainment most weekends, please call for details.

The Bearded Collie

Address: 234 Lakeshore Road East, Oakville
Telephone: 905-338-0050
Proprietor: Ann MacLeish
Opened: 1993
Bar: 12 Draft Taps

A long sit-down bar to the left as you enter runs almost half of the length of this narrow pub with a stand-up bar running parallel. An elevated dining area contains partitioned bench seating sections. A games room at the back of the bar has a pool table, shuffleboard and dartboards. Many items on the menu are homemade, including the burgers and meat pies; other traditional dishes include the excellent fish and chips. Thursday is half-price wing night and entertainment is provided on special occasions, please call for details.

Coach and Four

Address: 2432 Lakeshore Road West, Oakville
Telephone: 905-825-8940
General Manager: Derrick Dorsett
Opened: 1991
Bar: 10 Draft Taps

This traditional English-style pub has a tiled bar area and a carpeted dining section along with several comfortable booths. A small sit-down bar finds many regulars from the British Isles engaged in friendly banter. The walls are covered in an excellent collection of prints depicting mainly English themes. The menu is very much traditional fare with many daily and evening specials, and a large breakfast is offered on Saturday and Sundays between 11 AM and 3 PM. Thursday at the Coach is karaoke night.

Duck and Firkin

Address: 610 Ford Drive, Unit 5, Oakville
Telephone: 905-337-0330
Proprietors: Sandi and Krysty
Opened: 1999
Bar: 16 Draft Taps

The Duck is a friendly neighbourhood pub with a mix of booths and tables and an English-style décor. The pub has three pool tables and two dartboards along with the ever popular Golden Tee golf game to provide recreational use for its patrons. The Duck features a very varied menu from traditional to top-quality Canadian beef steaks. Daily specials include a pie, catch and pasta of the day, while Monday nights are wing nights. Tuesday the bar has tallboys on special and Wednesday is draft night with half-price appetizers.

The King's Arms

Address: 323 Church Street, Oakville
Telephone: 905-845-1010
Proprietors: Marco and Angelo
Opened: 1973
Bar: 12 Draft Taps

A large red brick building dating back almost a hundred years houses this very traditional English pub complete with carpeting throughout. An upstairs room is available for private parties as well as containing the pub's dartboards. The bar area has a couple of cozy booths with a separate pool room leading off to the side. The large menu contains traditional pub fare along with a good selection of burgers and sandwiches. Tuesday night has a wing and drinks special, Wednesday is the pizza party and Friday is fish and chip day. All-day breakfast special is available Sunday. Morgan every Thursday and Sunday features blues and 3 MDM on alternate weeks.

Finnegan's Wake

Address: 379 Speers Road, Oakville
Telephone: 905-815-9253
Proprietors: The Sannachan family
Opened: 2000
Bar: 14 Draft Taps

When arriving at Finnegan's Wake the mystical "tunnel entrance" transports you back in time and opens up to a historical journey of Ireland through the years. The private lower bar with its rich oak finish and Celtic carvings along with an illuminated glass bar top has a traditional feel with a modern flair; this bar is available for corporate functions and private parties. The main upper bar is shaped like a galleon ship encircling the gantry which houses a wide array of fine whiskies. The lounge has a sculpted Tara brooch covering most of the ceiling and a large replica "Rock of Kildare monument" encases a large three-sided fireplace. An alcove contains the "Braveheart" table with seating for eight in which the birthday boy or girl can feel like a king or queen for the evening. The menu features many fine Irish traditional dishes and also a selection of pizza and pasta. Entertainment Wednesday with the "One and Only" and Fridays with 3 MDM.

The Manchester Arms

Address: 2371 Lakeshore Road West, Oakville
Telephone: 905-825-4275
General Manager: Carole McKenzie
Opened: 1989
Bar: 13 Draft Taps

This small cozy pub in the Bronte district of Oakville has a row of booths each with their own low-hanging chandelier above the tables adding a warm and intimate setting to any meal. The bar is traditionally furnished and carpeted with authentic memorabilia throughout the pub. A traditional menu with fish and chips on special every Monday from 5 PM to 9 PM, Wednesday is jumbo wing night with the cajun wet being highly recommended and Saturday evenings features steak specials.

The Queen's Head

Address: 118 Dunn Street, Oakville.905-842-3070
Proprietor: Josephine Concannon
Opened: 1990
Telephone: 12Draft Taps

A large open British-style pub complete with Victorian décor, the walls are covered with a large fascinating collection of old country photographs and prints. The bar has a good selection of almost 30 single malts. A big-screen TV for all major sports and daily show-ings of *Coronation Street*. The main menu is very traditional with a large selection of finger-food appetizers. Daily lunch and dinner specials include an excellent prime rib. The Queen's Head is a busy weekend place where people go to socialize and converse without the distraction of loud music.

The Three Judges
Address: 176 Lakeshore Boulevard East, Oakville
Telephone: 905-849-7898
Proprietors: Opened under present management in 1999
Bar: 16 Draft Taps
A large stone central fireplace is the focal point of this traditional English-style pub in the heart of downtown Oakville. A large window gives a great view of the busy street and is perfect for people watching. The menu is traditional pub fare with a definite English flair and the bar is a very busy lunchtime spot due in part to its location but mostly to the excellent lunch specials. Friday night entertainment alternates between live bands and karaoke.

Orangeville

The Mad Hatter
Address: 82 Broadway, Orangeville
Telephone: 519-938-9709
Proprietor: Perry Meeker
Opened: 1997
Bar: 18 Draft Taps
Originally a feed mill in the 1880s, this historic building now houses a feed mill of another sort, the Mad Hatter. A large pub with a row of booths on the wall to the left as you go in and a long sit-down bar to the right. The bar boasts a collection of over two hundred silver tankards engraved with names of customers who have earned them by drinking a pint of every beer on tap over the course of the pub's anniversary week. Large sliding windows open up to the street and allow for a nice breeze to flow through the pub. A large billiards room is to the back, which also contains the big-screen TV. A large traditional/North American fare menu with many dinner specials. Live entertainment every Saturday night.

❖

The Winchester Arms

Address: 171 Broadway, Orangeville
Telephone: 519-941-9533
Proprietor: John Lee
Opened: 1994
Bar: 13 Draft Taps

A small pub with traditional décor and booths lining one wall and a window give this Winchester a cozy atmosphere. A backyard patio can be accessed through the designated dart area at the rear of the pub. The menu has a large selection of traditional along with regular pub fare. Monday kids eat free, Wednesday is wing night, Thursday is the curry special and Friday and Saturdays feature steak dinners. Entertainment is periodical so please call for details.

Orillia

The Blue Anchor

Address: 47 West Street South, Orillia
Telephone: 705-325-9977
Proprietor: Fay
Opened: 1996
Bar: 6 Draft Taps

A circular bar sits in the centre of this one-hundred-year-old converted textile mill. The interior walls still have the original brickwork including the wood-burning fireplace surround. Wooden floorboards complete the authentic look of yesteryear. The pub contains a pool table, shuffleboard and dartboards as well as an old piano that was donated by one of the customers. The pub is very community-focused and the regulars have many charity drives throughout the year. Every Sunday the pub hosts a dart competition where for a small entry fee patrons play for meat prizes; while you wait your turn have a game of free Sunday pool. The menu is pub fare and the drink prices are among the lowest in Ontario. Karaoke every Friday.

Finnegan's Irish Pub
Address: 480 West Street South, Orillia
Telephone: 705-323-9341
Proprietors: Jeff Watson, Amy Gritter and Gail Nyman
Opened: 1999
Bar: 12 Draft Taps
Dark wood with red carpeting and upholstery give this bar a very traditional look. The main-floor dining area is two rows of large booths bordering the bar giving it a secluded touch along with its own three tables. An upper-level dining section leads to the large patio, which covers the side and rear of the pub. There's a separate darts area by the bar and a pool table indoors as well as on the patio. The menu has a great cross-section ranging from traditional to pasta. Every day features clan-size nachos and a pitcher special. The bar is a featured venue in both the Orillia spring blues festival held four days every April and the Orillia jazz festival in October.

The Flock and Drover
Address: 85 Mississaga Street East, Orillia
Telephone: 705-323-9922
Proprietor: Jamie Miller
Opened: 1998
Bar: 13 Draft Taps
A narrow pub with a long sit-down bar running down the left and a row of booths lining the opposite wall. At the end of the bar there is an open dining section and an elevated area with bench seating. The walls are decorated with many soccer shirts and scarves that have been donated throughout the years. The pub has a novel way of raising funds for charity: it lets local businesses display their signs on the ceiling for a donation. A large menu with traditional fare and many daily specials, including all-you-can-eat mussels on Saturday and a 10 oz. prime rib dinner with Yorkshire pudding on Sunday. The wings are on special Monday to Thursday between 4 and 8 PM and all day Sunday to coincide with N.F.L. games. The bar also has the centre ice package showing most major hockey games. The bar has live bands every Friday and Saturday.

❖

The Fitzrichard Pub

Address: 575 Thornton Road North, Oshawa
Telephone: 905-438-1800
Proprietor: Rick Law
Opened: 1996
Bar: 16 Draft Taps

Located in the end unit of a plaza, the pub has plenty of parking. A large bright interior with an elevated bar level looking down to the dining area. A spectacular mural of a knight slaying a dragon takes up a whole wall at the far end of the pub. The pub also has a large-screen TV and dartboards. Lunch and dinner menu available; both contain a selection of traditional fare along with many daily specials, a separate kids' section is also contained in both. Entertainment weekly throughout the winter months and the last Wednesday of every month in the summer.

The Hare and Hound

Address: 15 Simcoe Street North, Oshawa
Telephone: 905-576-6139
Manager: Catherine Goodman
Opened: 1995
Bar: 17 Draft Taps

A friendly neighbourhood pub in the centre of downtown Oshawa. A pool table and dartboards for the energetic, or just relax and enjoy the friendly banter at the bar. An extensive menu includes traditional pub fare and an excellent chicken curry. There is an express lunch menu between 11 AM and 2 PM guaranteeing your meal will be served in 12 minutes or less. Sports teams should inquire with regards to specials. Acoustic and blues night open stage hosted on Sundays by Glen Bensley. On Friday nights the Hare and Hound's very own Angela Cain performs. Angela has her first C.D. being released January 2002.

Otter and Firkin

Address: 926 Simcoe Street North, Oshawa
Telephone: 905-436-9191
Proprietor: Hermia Tong
Opened: 2000
Bar: 16 Draft Taps

Located between Sunset Drive and Robert Street, the Otter is a traditional English pub with a warm and friendly environment. A pool table sits to the side of the bar area and the main floor has a mixture of booths and tables. Darts are available along with the Golden Tee golf game and the ever popular NTN trivia. A large varied menu with many daily specials. Wednesday is wing night and Thursday two can dine for $13.99, Saturday and Sunday kids eat free from 11:30 to 3 PM. Friday and Saturday night feature shooter specials.

The Tartan Tavern

Address: 555 Rossland Road East, Oshawa
Telephone: 905-728-9113
Proprietors: Bill Dolan and Kevin Kelly
Opened: 1978
Bar: 16 Draft Taps

As the name implies, this pub is as Scottish as it gets, from the tartan décor to the Glaswegian accents of the owners. There is a large back room available for parties with its own full bar for up to 75 people. The pub also has two pool tables. The menu has a large traditional pub fare section with the likes of haggis and black pudding. A Scottish breakfast is available daily along with brunch specials on Sundays. Wednesday night has mussels in a white wine and garlic sauce on special from 5 PM to close. Entertainment: Wednesday — Two for the Show; Thursday — Another Round; Friday — Deuce and The One and Only alternate. Saturday is all-day entertainment starting at 3 PM with George and Grace, karaoke with Carolyn at 6 PM to 10 PM and live bands from 10 PM to close. Sunday night is the One and Only.

The Thirsty Monk

Address: 36 Athol Street, Oshawa
Telephone: 905-728-3219
Opened: 1995
Bar: 17 Draft Taps

The area by the sit-down bar is a narrow passageway leading to the large backroom containing a pool table, big-screen TV and entertainment area. The pub also adjoins the Muse, a busy dance bar from Thursday to Saturday. The extensive menu includes many traditional and pasta dishes with the following evening specials: Sunday — Kids eat free; Monday — Two-for-one steak dinners; Tuesday — All you can eat spaghetti; Wednesday — Wings. Friday afternoon has complimentary roast beef sandwiches at the bar. Entertainment every Saturday with house band Men of Leisure.

The Waltzing Weasel

Address: 300 Taunton Road East, Oshawa
Telephone: 905-721-2533
Proprietor: Rob Sanderson
Opened: 1992
Bar: 15 Draft Taps

The sit-down bar is on an elevated level and at lunch time and cocktail hour it is very busy with a loyal regular crowd. The walls have hundreds of caricatures depicting staff and customers past and present so don't sit too long or you may find yourself up there with them. A wide selection of pub-style and contemporary food including a children's menu. There is a great "Munchies and Fun Stuff" section containing for the big appetite the "kitchen sink," which is probably better shared as it has half the menu in it. Monday is "suds and feather" night and Wednesday has the tallboy cans on special with complimentary sausages and buns. Everyday features a half-price appetizer at lunch time. Entertainment every other Saturday.

The Winchester Arms
Address: 540 King Street West, Oshawa
Telephone: 905-404-0238
General Manager: Bobbi Jones
Opened: 199
Bar: 13 Draft Taps

A very large bright dining room with the many bookcases giving the feeling of a large Victorian parlour. Up a few steps and there is a large pool room and dartboards. The menu is traditional pub fare and more with the following nightly specials: Monday — Fish and chips; Tuesday — Two-for-one pasta; Wednesday — Wing night; Thursday — Buy one meal and get one free; Saturday — Steak night; Sunday — Roast beef special. A separate kids' menu with a special treat from the toy chest when finished. In the winter months a jazz band performs every Saturday night.

The Winchester Arms
Address: 1210 Simcoe Street, Oshawa
Telephone: 905-438-9046
General Manager: Lisa Miller
Opened: 2000
Bar: 12 Draft Taps

A fine selection of antiques adorn this tastefully decorated pub, including a magnificent antique dresser that is the focal point of the north dining room. A packet of crisps from England is available at the bar along with a selection of single malts. The menu is varied with the following evening specials: Monday — Suds and feathers; Tuesday — Two-for-one T-bone steaks; Wednesday — Wings; Thursday — Buy one meal and get one free; Friday — Fish and chips, Saturday: Steak night; Sunday — Roast beef and Yorkshire pudding. Free roast beef on a bun every Friday 4 PM to 6 PM at the bar only. Entertainment periodical, please call for details.

The Barley Mow

Address: 1060 Bank Street, Ottawa
Telephone: 613-730-1279/**Web:** http://www.barleymow.com
Proprietors: Gary, Suzanne and Jason
Opened: 199
Bar: 18 Draft Taps

The Barley Mow takes great pride in being a place where people come to talk and socialize and therefore shies away from loud music and big-screen TVs. Not sure of what draft to drink? Ask for the draft train sampler where you can choose five five-oz. drafts of your choice for the price of a pint. This great sampling idea can also be used for single malts, of which there are 40 to choose from. Trivia nights are held every Monday and are open to teams or individuals. The menu has traditional fare and also a few exotic Malaysian selections. The fish and chips are also a pub favourite and are served in newspaper just like in the old country. Wings are on special Monday and Tuesday 4 PM to close.

The Brig

Address: 23 York Street, Ottawa
Telephone: 613-562-6666
General Manager: Kevin Kelly
Opened: 1993
Bar: 17 Draft Taps

This busy market bar hosts patio parties every Thursday, Friday and Saturday nights in the summer along with the very popular shooter girls. The front of the bar opens onto the street, allowing the sights and the sounds of the busy summer nights entry into the pub. With the change of seasons there is a large stone fireplace that heats up the whole bar. In the winter this pub plays host to Molson Extreme teams on Wednesday nights, a night full of Molson promotions and giveaways. The menu is a traditional/ Canadian mix. Food and drink specials every Sunday night.

Clocktower Brew Pub

Address: 575 Bank Street, Ottawa
Telephone: 613-233-7849
Brewmaster: John Coughlan
Opened: 1996
Bar: 13 Draft Taps

The actual brewing process can be viewed through large windows from the bar. A number of large, comfortable circular booths are perfect for business lunch meetings. Downstairs has a full bar with pool tables and a large fireplace that can be booked for private functions. The in-house brews include cask-conditioned and sea-sonal favourites such as raspberry wheat. They also have a good selection of single malts. The menu is an excellent cross-section ranging from fish and chips to teriyaki salmon. Take-out is available and the Brew pub will also cater your event. Tuesday is wing night and appetizers are half price 3 PM to 7 PM Monday to Thursday.

The Cock and Lion

Address: 202 Sparks Street, Ottawa
Telephone: 613-233-0080
Proprietors: David and Howard Appotibe
Opened: 2000
Bar: 24 Draft Taps

This bar is a few steps down from the street and has soft lighting to give a very warm atmosphere. There are large chairs and couches surrounding candle-lit tables along with fireplaces scattered throughout to add to this relaxing ambience. A small but good selection of single malts available. The menu is mainly North American pub fare with daily wing and nacho specials. Entertainment from Tuesday to Saturday ranges from jazz to r&b with Thursday being reserved for karaoke. The Cock and Lion also owns a pool hall next door with seven tables.

D'Arcy McGees

Address: 44 Sparks Street, Ottawa
Telephone: 613-230-4433
General Manager: Jeff O'Reilly
Opened: 1997
Bar: 16 Draft Taps

Named after Thomas D'Arcy McGee, one of the founding fathers of Confederation who was assassinated on Sparks Street in 1868. The bar was designed and hand crafted in Wexford, Southern Ireland, before being shipped over. Voted best pub by Ottawa Sun readers in 2000. Located in the busy pedestrian thoroughfare known as the Sparks Street Mall, this pub is very popular with local government employees and tourists alike. The bar takes up the centre of the room with several separate areas leading off from the main floor, each with quaint little booths separated by glass and wood partitions. A selection of cigars is available on sale from the cigar cabinet. The bar carries over 20 types of fine Irish whiskey. A large menu with a good selection of traditional fare. Live entertainment Friday and Saturday nights.

The Double Decker Pub

Address: 62 William Street, Ottawa
Telephone: 613-241-0066
General Manager: Sim
Opened: 1994
Bar: 18 Draft Taps

Sitting atop the lower deck diner, this pub offers a great view of the busy Byward Market. The booths contain actual bus seats along with slide-open windows. A long bar provides plenty of seats for the N.T.N. trivia crowd. The far end of the bar contains a pool table and video games. A pub menu with an excellent sizzle and grill section. Tuesday and Wednesday are wing nights and on Friday from 4 PM to 7 PM the bar has free appetizers. Open early on Saturday and Sunday for breakfast.

The Duke of Somerset

Address: 352 Somerset Street West, Ottawa
Telephone: 613-233-7762/**Web:** www.dukeofsomerset.com
Proprietor: Edgar Mitchell
Opened: 1965
Bar: 16 Draft Taps

Majestic Somerset House, built in 1898, is where this well-known Ottawa bar is based. The downstairs traditional pub has been a favourite hang-out for rugby and soccer fans for many years. The upstairs houses a large tavern that has been on the corner of Bank and Somerset for over 60 years. A lovely side patio on the heritage streetscape of Somerset Village has a large green double decker bus as a backdrop. The pub also has a pool table and is home to several dart teams. The menu features many traditional dishes and daily specials; Monday nights the wings are on special from 4 PM until 8 PM. Live entertainment every Friday and Saturday nights.

❖

The Elephant and Castle
Address: 50 Rideau Street, Ottawa
Telephone: 613-234-5544
Proprietors: Corporate
Opened: 1983
Bar: 14 Draft Taps

Located in the Rideau Centre Mall, this well-known pub is a welcome break from the hustle of this busy shopping centre. On two levels the décor of this pub is reminiscent of Tudor-style with the large beams criss-crossing the ceiling. The excellent collection of pub memorabilia was shipped over from England and the chairs are based on authentic London pub furnishings. Very popular with tourists, one can also book a canal tour with the staff and the Elephant and Castle will cater the event. The menu contains a large selection of traditional pub fare with a good selection of finger foods. Recommended are the fish and chips.

Grace O'Malley's
Address: 1541 Merrivale Road, Ottawa
Telephone: 613-226-9695
Proprietor: Patrick Akeson
Opened: 1998
Bar: 12 Draft Taps,

This large pub has authentic wooden floors and a long sit-down bar. A stage area and dance floor sit central among the many booths and tables. The artifacts were picked up in local junkyards and auctions and even include cemetery railings, which now surround a booth. Watch for the flaming lampshades above the bar. A good selection of single malts. The menu is a mix of traditional and Canadian pub fare. Wing specials on Tuesday nights. Entertainment as follows: Monday is open stage, Tuesday is the house band and Wednesday to Saturday it's live bands featuring the best in Celtic and Maritime music.

The Heart and Crown

Address: 67 Clarence Street, Ottawa
Telephone: 613-562-0674
Proprietors: Larry and Pat
Opened: 1992
Bar: 16 Draft Taps

A traditional Irish pub with many of the staff hailing from Ireland. There is a large covered courtyard patio and a large snug with its own bar which are available for private parties. The menu is traditional Irish pub fare with the classic pub plate being one of the favourites — a hearty serving of sausages, bacon, home fries, beans and toast. Entertainment Wednesday to Saturday features live Celtic music. An authentic Irish pub atmosphere with both owners coming from the Emerald Isle.

Lieutenant's Pump

Address: 361 Elgin Street, Ottawa
Telephone: 613-238-2949
Proprietor: John Clouse
Opened: 1984
Bar: 12 Draft Taps

The main bar is at the front of the building and hosts a big-screen TV, pool table, shuffleboard and dartboards. For those who like a quieter setting the lounge aptly named the Queen's Room is located at the back. The menu gets away from traditional pub fare and for many it is a welcome change to partner their pint of Guinness. A good selection of pastas and a favourite is the Thai green curry chicken. However on Sunday the Pump has a traditional roast beef dinner. The bar has a varied collection of single malts. The patio faces west and is a virtual sun trap for those who like it hot.

The Manx

Address: 370 Elgin Street, Ottawa
Telephone: 613-231-2070
Proprietors: Chris and Robin
Opened: 1993
Bar: 17 Draft Taps

A few steps down from street level this small bar is probably one of the best kept secrets in Ottawa. The Manx takes its selection of single malt whiskies seriously and highlights a daily malt special to introduce the spirit to newcomers and experts alike. The walls are decorated with the works of local artists and these showcases are changed monthly. The menu is small but contains such dishes as the Sri Lankan wrap which contains lamb curry, roasted mushrooms and cheddar in a flour tortilla. A different menu is available for Saturday and Sunday brunch. Entertainment Sunday and Monday nights featuring live music.

Mayflower

Address: 247 Elgin Street, Ottawa
Telephone: 613-238-3731
General Manager: Bob Jones
Opened: 1979
Bar: 14 Draft Taps

One of the first authentic British-style pubs in Ottawa, this bar still caters to most of its original clientele. Fairly small with nautical memorabilia decorating the walls it is reminiscent of the small pubs back in Britain during the 50s and early 60s. A selection of 14 single malts can be had and the menu is a mixed selection of sandwiches and pub fare. The Mayflower also owns the diner next door which is a very popular breakfast spot.

Mayflower II

Address: 201 Queen Street, Ottawa
Telephone: 613-238-1138
General Manager: Marty Waugh
Opened: 1979
Bar: 16 Draft Taps

Like its sister pub one of the first British-style pubs in Ottawa. This pub is a flight of stairs up from the main street and has a narrow interior with a long sit-down bar. The seats at the window offer a great view down to the street below. The walls are a nautical theme with plenty of sea-faring items scattered throughout the pub. The bar carries over 40 types of bottled beer both domestic and imported along with 27 single malts. A large pub fare menu. Tuesday and Wednesday are wing nights and Thursday is the nachos and chili special. Entertainment on St. Patrick's Day.

Patty Bolands

Address: 101 Clarence Street, Ottawa
Telephone: 613-789-7822
General Manager: Michael Hannas
Opened: 2000
Bar: 20 Draft Taps

This large Irish-style pub contains a snug bar as well as a full bar upstairs. The main bar has a mirrored backdrop with a cherry wood surround that gives an old-fashioned authenticity to its Irish theme. There are four fireplaces throughout the bar, including a natural stone surround fireplace set in the snug. The large upstairs can be booked for private parties. The menu is varied with traditional Irish favourites including boxty, a potato pancake rolled and stuffed with a savoury filling. The pub also boasts a carvery which adds that special touch to weekend brunches. Entertainment Thursday, Friday and Saturday featuring the best of live Celtic music.

Patty's Pub

Address: 1186 Bank Street, Ottawa
Telephone: 613-730-2434
Proprietor: Art
Opened: 1997
Bar: 17 Draft Taps

The pillars and flooring of this Irish-style bar are all from old barns and along with the large two-sided stone fireplace give it the look of an old country pub. There is a small room with one table called the Dublin Snug that is perfect for that quiet romantic drink. The draft cider is poured from an actual 1960 fire hydrant atop the bar. Menu is a traditional/Canadian mix with many daily specials. Celtic entertainment every Thursday night and during the fall and winter live bands Fridays and Saturdays. An all-day bash on a very busy St. Patrick's Day.

Royal Oak

Address: 318 Bank Street, Ottawa
Telephone: 613-236-0190
Opened: 1980
Bar: 18 Draft Taps

This is the original Royal Oak and sits at the busy corner of Bank and Somerset. The pub is made up of three large rooms each with windows opening up to the street. The bar is always busy at lunchtime and has a very loyal clientele after business hours. The menu is a traditional/North American mix and a separate snack menu is also available all day until close. The following are the evening specials: Monday — Broccoli and cheddar poppers; Tuesday — Beef enchiladas; Wednesday — Spring rolls; Thursday — Nachos; Friday — Fish and chips and Sunday features a roast beef dinner special. Entertainment is periodical so please call for details.

Royal Oak

Address: 1217 Wellington Street, Ottawa
Telephone: 613-728-6661
General Manager: Peter
Opened: 2000
Bar: 16 Draft Taps

This Royal Oak is panelled in rich, dark mahogany and has an impressive oval-shaped bar. Lighting is a highlight of the interior as two sides have floor-to-ceiling glass walls and there are two glass garage doors that open up to the L-shaped patio. Located in the west end of Ottawa in an area where new residential construction is bringing in more people to the neighbourhood, this pub will be a welcome addition to their new surroundings. The menu is varied with Saturday and Mondays featuring a wing special, while fish and chips are the order of the day on Friday. Entertainment is periodical so please call for details.

Royal Oak

Address: 2067 Meadowbrook Road, Gloucester
Telephone: 613-741-0072
General Manager: Alvin
Opened: 1994
Bar: 16 Draft Taps

Located in the city of Gloucester in the east of Ottawa, this friendly pub is a popular lunchtime spot for local office employees. The décor provides a cozy atmosphere and is richly appointed with oak-paneled walls hung with antique British Railway posters. Situated across from Pineview Golf Club it is the perfect meeting place for golfers leaving the 18th green. A large patio offers relaxing summer afternoons. The menu contains many traditional dishes and the wings are on special every Monday, Tuesday and Saturday. A weekend brunch is served between 11 AM and 2 PM Entertainment every second Friday.

Royal Oak

Address: 161 Laurier Avenue East, Ottawa
Telephone: 613-230-9233
General Manager: Ken
Opened: 1987
Bar: 16 Draft Taps

Recently renovated to allow for the increase in business this Royal Oak sits on the edge of the University of Ottawa campus and attracts a mature student crowd and local Sandy Hill residents. The pub is very popular at lunchtimes with local office workers, students and university staff. A beautiful patio overlooks adjacent church gardens and adds a touch of serenity while taking a break from the books. A large varied menu with many daily specials, with wings on special every Tuesday and Saturday. Entertainment is periodical so please call for details.

Royal Oak

Address: 779 Bank Street, Ottawa
Telephone: 613-235-2624
General Manager: Tammy
Opened: 1991
Bar: 16 Draft Taps

Located in an area of the city known as the Glebe, a prime residential and shopping area and also close to the Carleton University campus, this pub serves as a student gathering place as well as being a neighbourhood pub with a varied clientele. The menu is a good mix of traditional and North American fare with many lunch and evening specials. Wings are featured every Sunday, Monday and Tuesday. The pub features live entertainment every Saturday night.

Royal Oak

Address: 1981 St. Joseph Boulevard, Orleans
Telephone: 613-834-9005
General Manager: Rick Boland
Opened: 1998
Bar: 16 Draft Taps

This pub features a large brick fireplace, large wooden beams across the ceiling and beautiful hardwood floors. The interior is very reminiscent of an old country pub. A large patio seating almost 90 is a great place to watch the world go by on the corner of Jeanne D'Arc. Open only a couple of years, it has already become the "local" for the residents of Orleans. A traditional/North American menu with the wings on special every Sunday, Monday and Tuesday. Weekends feature a brunch buffet between 9 AM and 1 PM. Entertainment twice a month, please call for details.

Royal Oak

Address: 221 Echo Drive, Ottawa
Telephone: 613-234-3700
General Manager: Chris
Opened: 2001
Bar: 16 Draft Taps

This beautiful new addition to the Royal Oak family sits by the canal at Pretoria Bridge. There is a great two-tiered patio allowing the best of outdoor viewing in this mature setting. The upstairs dining room is available for private parties and a fabulous table d'hôte is served there every Thursday, Friday and Saturday. Downstairs has another dining room off to the side. A mixed menu containing many traditional dishes and daily specials, including a pasta special every Thursday night. Every Sunday and Monday nights the pub has wing and draft specials to coincide with the big football games.

❖

The Tara Cross

Address: 263 Bank Street, Ottawa
Telephone: 613-237-9493
Proprietor: Calum MacKenzie
Opened: 1993
Bar: 16 Draft Taps

Large windows flank this corner bar to give a bright interior as well as great people-watching seats in the busy Bank Street area. Very soccer orientated, this pub carries all major soccer events on the big screen. A small snug with seating for 12 was originally an bank vault. There is a function room available for private parties and at the time of writing a games room was soon to be added. The menu is a mixture of traditional and North American fare. Wednesday is wing night. Live entertainment Friday and Saturday nights.

Woody's

Address: 330 Elgin Street, Ottawa
Telephone: 613-567-1088
Proprietor: Jason
Opened: 1995
Bar: 25 Draft Taps

This bar opens early to serve breakfast every day and is a popular spot in winter for many Rideau skaters. The bar features many microbreweries and specialty coffees. There is a large-screen TV for all major sporting events with comfortable seating in the dining lounge. In the summer the windows open onto the street. There is a fireplace in the main bar and also in the corner of the dining area. A good selection of single malts. Menu is a cross between pub fare, pastas and a selection of seven stir fries. Tuesday is two-for-one pizza night and Wednesday is wing night. Appetizers are two-for-one between 4 PM and 7 PM Monday to Saturday.

The Crown and Thistle

Address: 71 Foster Street, Perth
Telephone: 613-267-4748
Proprietors: Wendy and David Kirkbright
Opened: 1991
Bar: 14 Draft Taps

This neighbourhood pub treats its regulars like family. The bar only sells draft beers and ciders, and publican Dave prides himself on the quality of his pints. A good selection of single malts is available also. A little memorabilia shop offers pub collectibles, and a monthly pub newsletter announces upcoming events and specials. A large traditional pub menu with homemade pies and cornish pasties. Wednesday nights are very popular, with a two-for-one fish and chip special. You can catch Britain's favourite soap, Coronation Street, on the telly and enjoy a hearty meal every Sunday from 11 AM. Later in the day the special is a traditional roast beef dinner with Yorkshire pudding. Entertainment every Thursday night.

Peterborough

Peterborough Arms

Address: 300 Charlotte Street, Peterborough
Telephone: 705-876-0306
Proprietor: Tim Burke
Opened: 1991
Bar: 20 Draft Taps

Before you enter the Arms you have to pass the biggest patio in town with seating for almost 180; the patio is also heated for maximum outdoor use. The pub consists of two large rooms, the bar area, with a darts room off to the side, and a separate dining section. The Arms has the most micro brews of anyone in town and these are especially popular with the student clientele. The menu is a mix of traditional and North American fare with wings on special every Monday night, and all-you-can-eat spaghetti and meatballs on Tuesdays. Monday is also movie night on the big screen. Wednesday night features Peterborough's biggest open stage. Sunday afternoon has a 10-year tradition of Celtic music featuring the Reverend Ken and Sunday evening is an acoustic rock session from 9 until close.

❖

Riley' Olde Towne Pub

Address: 2253 George Street, Peterborough
Proprietors: The Kakouros family
Opened: 2000
Bar: 19 Draft Taps

At the back of this bar is a lounge with large couches, easy chairs and a gas fireplace, making it the perfect place to sit back and relax with your pint and paper. The sit-down bar is at least 30 feet long and a stand-up bar just as long runs parallel. There are plenty of booths throughout the pub with a few seating only two, which makes for a quiet lunch or dinner with your partner. Next door with an adjoining entrance is a 20-table pool hall with a full-service bar. At the time of writing Riley's was in the process of adding an upstairs night club and rooftop patio. Menu has an international flair with traditional, Italian, Greek and Texmex. Entertainment on Tuesday, Thursday, Friday and Saturday nights.

Pickering

The Harp and Crown

Address: 300 Kingston Road, Pickering
Telephone: 905-509-6565/**Web:** http://www.harpandcrown.com
Proprietors: John Morgan and Tom Rogers
Opened: 1998
Bar: 26 Draft Taps

This bar has two large rooms — the non-smoking Crown dining room, which can also be booked for private functions (smoking or non-smoking optional), and the bar itself with its own large dining area and warm décor. A good selection of single malts and an exceptional selection of draft beers including a couple of micro breweries. The menu is a traditional/North American mix with the following evening specials: Sunday, Monday and Tuesday are wing nights; Monday — Ribs; Tuesday — Mussels; Wednesday — Steak. Entertainment every Thursday, Friday and Saturday.

❖

The Fox Mansion
Address: 1294 Kingston Rd., Pickering
Telephone: 905-831-1000
Bar: 20 Draft Taps

The Old Liverpool House, which today is the Fox Mansion, was built in 1827, and is a Pickering landmark. Originally a private residence, the building became a hotel, with Sir John A. MacDonald its most well-known guest. In the 1960s, the building was moved to its present location, and after careful restoration was re-opened as the Fox and Fiddle. The pub serves a mixed menu of traditional pub fare, such as steak and kidney pie, and North American favourites like chicken fingers and stir fries. For a fancier meal there is steak, prime rib, scampi, and rack of lamb. A Lunch Express menu is available from 11 to 3 PM during the work week, as well as half-price appetizers from 4 to 6. Tuesdays it's 30-cent wings, on Wednesdays indulge in sizzling fajitas for half price, and on Thursday there's the T-bone platter special, as well as dancing and karaoke. Watch football on the big-screen TV on Sundays and Mondays, and enjoy the dancing upstairs on Fridays and Saturdays, with music by the d.j.

Broghan's Lane

Address: 22 Ontario Street, Port Hope
Telephone: 905-885-9557
Proprietor: Sean Sheehan
Opened: 1998
Bar: 13 Draft Taps

This Irish-owned pub sees visitors from Ireland coming back again and again, as the hospitality is friendly and genuine. The walls feature the works of local artists and large prints of yachts grace the non-smoking dining room. The upstairs room is available for private functions. A small rooftop patio offers a view of the Ganaraska River. The menu is mostly traditional and during the week a working mans lunch is on at a special price. Monday night is an all-you-can-eat fish fry and wings are on special Wednesdays. Entertainment is periodical, please call for details.

The Winchester Arms

Address: 299 Ridout Street, Port Hope
Telephone: 905-885-9393
Manager: Ryan Jones
Opened: 2000
Bar: 12 Draft Taps

This attractive bar has the look of a large solarium from the outside due to its large window frontage. There is a small separate darts room where novices can practice in safety. A golf course lies behind the Winchester, so what a perfect way to end a day on the links by enjoying a pint in the pub. Menu is a traditional/North American mix. Monday is wing night from 4 PM to 10 PM, Tuesday is pasta night from 5 PM to 9 PM, Wednesday kids eat free (from kids menu), Thursday is fish and chip night, Saturday is steak night and Sunday sees a special roast beef dinner from 4 PM to 10 PM. Complimentary munchies Friday from 4 PM to 6 PM. Wings are half-price every night 9 PM until close.

Jester's Court

Address: 279 Queen Street, Port Perry
Telephone: 905-985-2775
Proprietors: Jeff and Deena
Opened: 1997
Bar: 13 Draft Taps

Built in 1859 and then renovated as a hotel in 1865, this grand old building sits on Port Perry's historic main street. The hotel has long gone but some guests from these early days are still around and most of the staff can testify to objects being moved around by these mischievous ghosts. The downstairs dining room has a large fireplace and numerous booths while the sit-down bar area is in a separate room to the left as you enter. An upstairs room with all the charm of a traditional lounge can be used for private functions, seating up to 55 people. The pub has won many local awards, including best restaurant, with the menu serving an array of traditional dishes; the prime rib dinner is excellent.

Richmond Hill

Falcon and Firkin

Address: 10300 Yonge Street, Richmond Hill
Telephone: 905-883-4253
Proprietor: Mike Lewicki
Opened: 1992
Bar: 16 Draft Taps

A large L-shaped bar sits in the middle of the pub with a section of booths to the rear. Three pool tables, three mega touch games and two Golden Tee golf games provide plenty of entertainment for customers. A large menu featuring traditional dishes and many daily specials. Wing nights are Monday through Wednesday and the popular "two can dine for $12.99" special is available Tuesday and Sunday evenings. The Falcon has a large Yonge Street patio and runs many promotions. The bar features ongoing sports coverage on its two big-screen TVs. A disc jockey plays every Thursday and a jam session is on Saturdays. Sunday night is busy with a disc jockey and karaoke.

❖

Fox and Fiddle

Address: 115 York Boulevard, Richmond Hill
Telephone: 905-886-0637
General Manager: Sherri Groves
Opened: 1989
Bar: 22 Draft Taps

Situated in the midst of Richmond Hill's high tech area, this bar is the businessman's dream, with excellent food and old world charm — it's the perfect after-work retreat. A large dance floor is central to the pub while a dining area off to the side provides plenty of booths for a more intimate atmosphere. The bar area itself has a long sit-down bar with a games room containing many large video screens. A small section of booths also lines the wall as you enter the pub. The menu includes many traditional dishes and a good selection of sandwiches and wraps as well as the following evening specials: Monday — 15% discount off food; Tuesday — wings; Wednesday — two-for-one fajitas. The Fox and Fiddle also has many daily homemade specials. Entertainment has a jam night on Tuesday while Wednesday to Saturday the best of today's music by popular d.j.'s.

King Henry's Arms
Address: 9301 Yonge Street, Unit 2a, Richmond Hill
Telephone: 905-787-0900
Proprietor: Alan Cockburn
Opened: 2000
Bar: 20 Draft Taps

The bar area is to the right when you enter this cozy traditional English-style pub and to the left is an upper-level area lined with comfortable booths. The walls are adorned with many fine English-theme prints. The pub shows all major soccer games and is rumoured to have the best chicken wings in Richmond Hill. Located in a large mall, there is plenty of parking. A traditional pub fare menu and more has Monday night wing specials, Tuesday night patio barbecues changing to seafood night in the winter, and half-price mussels on Thursday. Saturday is the popular prime rib dinner. Also for "dessert" the only place around to have a deep-fried Mars bar. Karaoke and drink specials every Tuesday.

Limerick's Irish Pub
Address: 10720 Yonge Street, Richmond Hill
Telephone: 905-883-6696
Proprietor: Lance Anderson
Opened: 1998
Bar: 15 Draft Taps

Located in the north end of Richmond Hill, the Dublin accent behind the bar and the green décor let you know that you are in an Irish pub. Most of the menu is freshly made on the premises and includes traditional Irish dishes. A daily happy hour of food specials runs from 4 PM until 7 PM. Other specials include Tuesday — Half-price wings; Thursday — Two-for-one pasta and Sunday — Prime rib dinner. Entertainment Thursday, Friday and Saturday, with Thursdays featuring well-known entertainer Lou Moore. St. Patrick's Day sees an all-day celebration featuring Irish dancers, live bands and food specials.

London Pub Co

Address: 9724 Yonge Street, Richmond Hill
Telephone: 905-508-2770
Proprietors: Mauro and Kevin
Opened: 2000
Bar: 16 Draft Taps

Located on the main strip, the London Pub was built on the look and feel of a true authentic English pub. Relax and feel at home in a cozy atmosphere, whether at the bar, on the patio, in the dining room or the Royal Lounge. A full lunch and dinner menu is offered with excellent business lunch specials daily. Along with the many draft beers are a large variety of wines and liquers. Karaoke, live jams and entertainment are also offered weekly, so come in, unwind and experience the heritage and hospitality on tap.

❖

McDuffs

Address: 9555 Yonge Street, Richmond Hill
Telephone: 905-770-9105
Proprietor: Alan Comrie
Opened: 1995
Bar: 9 Draft Taps

Scottish soccer shirts and scarves along with other Scottish memorabilia adorn the walls of this wee Scottish pub. Landlord Alan Comrie with his flaming red hair and handlebar mustache is always on hand to share a story or joke. The menu is traditionally Scottish with the likes of square sausage adding to an excellent Scottish breakfast. Entertainment is every Friday and Saturday where the regulars are always encouraged to get up and sing. Sunday afternoon has featured performers from 4 PM to 8 PM.

Beaver and Firkin

Address: 16 Lebovic Avenue, Scarborough
Telephone: 416-615-5558
Proprietor: Sandra Liberty
Opened: 2000
Bar: 16 Draft Taps

The main bar area is a mixture of booths and tables with a pool table off to the side. A back room can be used for larger groups and is especially popular for Christmas parties. This cozy English-style pub is located opposite a large movie theatre and on Tuesday nights patrons bring in their movie ticket and receive a discount on entrees. The menu is large and varied with many excellent daily specials. Monday nights are wing nights. The NTN trivia is available at the bar along with a friendly game of darts. Wednesday is Martini night for the ladies.

The Doghouse

Address: 2256 Kingston Road, Scarborough
Telephone: 416-264-3092
Proprietors: Patrick Roine and Terry Navickas
Opened: 2000
Bar: 9 Draft Taps

A small pub with a brick interior and a small sit-down bar. The walls are decorated with many interesting black and white photographs depicting the bygone days of Ireland and Liverpool. A large-screen TV for all major soccer games. Patrick and Terry have tried to keep this pub as realistic and traditional as possible and they have succeeded — it is like stepping back to the small northern pubs of the 40s and 50s. Traditional pub fare, with many homemade items including meat pies. Entertainment monthly, please call for details.

Mahoney's Pub

Address: 3676 St. Clair Avenue East, Scarborough
Telephone: 416-261-0326
Proprietors: Martin Mahoney and Ken Vandermay
Opened: 2000
Bar: 16 Draft Taps

Located in the busy St. Clair area, this pub is unique in that its backyard patio overlooks a driving range and small park giving it a country feel in downtown Scarborough. Big-screen TV, dartboards and a fireplace finish off the cozy lounge. A good selection of single malts and Irish whiskies. Big annual summer patio party, call for details. Other events include St. Patrick's Day and New Year's Eve. Menu is traditional pub fare with wing nights on Thursday. Entertainment weekly.

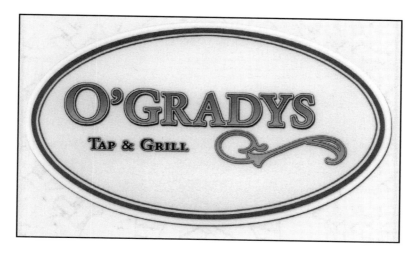

O'Grady's

Address: 2167 Victoria Park, Scarborough
Telephone: 416-449-9371
General Manager: Jackie
Opened: 1996
Bar: 12 Draft Taps

O'Grady's was around the corner on Ellesmere before moving to present location in 1996 and has had a loyal clientele for many years. Deceptively small from the front, this bar is impressively large with three sections that get larger as you proceed through the pub. A large games room at the back contains four pool tables, dartboards and a big-screen TV. The middle section is where the entertainment is, with a dance floor and tables and also a giant pull-down screen. The long sit-down bar stretches two-thirds of the way through the pub and the regulars sitting there hail from all over, including many from the British Isles. The menu is a good mix, with plenty of traditional fare. Wings are half-price Monday, Wednesday and Sunday nights. A jazz band alternates every Saturday with a d.j. Karaoke is on Tuesday and live bands on the Friday.

Olde Stone Cottage Inn
Address: 3750 Kingston Road, Scarborough
Telephone: 416-265-7932
Proprietors: Fred, Anthony, Padraig and Tony
Opened: 2001
Bar: 20 Draft Taps

This beautiful old country cottage is like stepping back in time when you enter the bar with its rustic interior and fireplaces. There is a small cozy snug in the corner and the sit-down bar is filled with friendly regulars. The back room however brings you back to modern times with the new sports room extension containing a pool table, dartboards and big-screen TVs showing all the big soccer and rugby games and the occasional Gaelic games. A large patio wraps around the front and side of the cottage. A private function room is available upstairs catering to 60. Irish traditional menu and more with homemade pies. Entertainment on a regular basis and a dinner show every six weeks, please call for details.

The Prince George
Address: 781 Warden Avenue, Scarborough
Telephone: 416-751-9740
Proprietor: George Gervas
Opened: 1972
Bar: 10 Draft Taps

The Prince George sits in what was an old munitions building and uses the old escape tunnels, which were for use in case of explosions, as storage rooms. This large open bar has a 40-foot-long sit-down bar running along one side of the room. There is a pool table and a total of nine dartboards along the far wall. The pub has very reasonable beer prices which are more in common with club pricing. North American fare with many daily specials. The pub is part of the Embers restaurant which has dining and banquet facilities. Live entertainment every Friday night.

Purdy's Pub

Address: 6091 Kingston Road, Scarborough
Telephone: 416-281-3680
Proprietor: Eric Purdy
Opened: 1999
Bar: 14 Draft Taps

This small friendly neighbourhood pub has a traditional Irish feel to it, with many prints and posters depicting the Emerald Isle. The small sit-down bar is to the left as you go in with the main floor area to the right, a small snug is tucked away towards the window side behind the front door. A backyard patio has just been added as well a full bar downstairs complete with a dart area. Every June sees a big beer tent in the car park during Heritage Day. A traditional pub menu with two-for-one wings every Monday night. Live bands every weekend.

The Tara Inn

Address: 2365 Kingston Road, Scarborough
Telephone: 416-266-6200
Proprietors: Wayne and Maria Reddy
Opened: 1993
Bar: 15 Draft Taps

The menu states that the Tara was started by an Irish prizefighter who loved to sing and a Ukranian farm girl from Saskatchewan. The result for the people of Scarborough is a fine community meeting place with good food, good service and an Irish atmosphere that speaks for itself. A few steps down to the bar area where at the weekend its standing room only. The dining areas feature many booths and a big-screen TV for all major sporting events. There is a separate pool room which also includes a table top football game. Menu is a good mix with everything from pizza to roti; there is also a large selection with a definite Irish flair. Karaoke on the last Saturday of each month and jam nights periodically. Present management are the son and daughter-in-law of the singing fighter and the prairie princess.

❖

The Tara Inn

Address: 2609 Eglinton Avenue East, Scarborough
Telephone: 416-264-2723
Proprietor: Derek
Opened: 1988
Bar: 16 Draft Taps

The original Tara and sister pub to the Kingston Road location. A small traditional Irish bar with many of the locals originally from the old country. The sit-down bar is to your right as you enter and to your left the wall is lined with comfortable booths. Interesting Irish memorabilia adorn the walls of this very cozy local. A large-screen TV is at the back of the pub and the dartboards are up front by the window. A large 50-gallon fish tank sits behind the bar and unlike Chinese restaurants the fish are not on the menu. The menu is a good mix with the emphasis on traditional Irish fare. An all-day Irish breakfast is especially popular on Sunday when the Tara opens at 10 AM. The wings are by far, according to regulars, the best in Scarborough and they can be had at a special price every Wednesday night. Two-for-one pasta is the Thursday special. Monday is euchre night and entertainment is provided every Sunday and most weekends during winter months.

Never Miss an Old Firm Game!

Toronto Branch of the Glasgow Celtic Supporters Club
2220 Midland Ave., Unit 27, Scarborough
Tel: 416-609-8819; President: Billy McCormack

Toronto Branch of the Glasgow Rangers Supporters Club
1950 Ellesmere Rd., Unit 7, Scarborough
Tel: 416-439-0650; President: Jack Buchanan

Dr. Dillane's Pub and Patio

Address: 226 Main Street, Schomberg
Telephone: 905-939-7151
Proprietors: Kit and Anna Andrew
Opened: 1994
Bar: 12 Draft Taps

Located in a wooden heritage building in historical downtown
Schomberg, this was once the home and practice of Dr. Morris
Dillane, the town doctor until his demise in 1956. When first
opened the pub was only licensed for 15, making it at the time the
smallest pub in Ontario. Since then the house has been taken over
bit by bit; first a billiard room was added and soon a non-smoking
dining room will add to the charm of this unique village pub. The
floor in the small bar slopes dramatically to one side giving the
impression you have had one too many. The garden patio is
absolutely splendid in summer adding a beautiful backdrop to
your lunchtime pint. The pub hosts an annual anniversary party
which is locally famous and it is standing room only. Menu is a
varied collection featuring an excellent shepherd's pie. The fries are
freshly cut and are great on their own. Entertainment is periodical,
please call for details.

❖

The Earl of Whitchurch

Address: 6204 Main Street, Stouffville
Telephone: 905-640-8300
Proprietors: Steve and Melissa
Opened: 2001
Bar: 16 Draft Taps

The Earl sits in a majestic old home just by the railway tracks on the busy Stouffville main street. The small sit-down bar is to the right as you enter and the dining area straight on with its comfortable seating and cozy fireplace. The back patio is shaded by a number of mature trees. The upstairs, like the downstairs, is traditionally furnished and carpeted and is used for entertainment and theme nights. The menu contains traditional and North American fare with the following evening specials: Monday — Mussels; Tuesday — Half-price wings; Wednesday — Pasta; Thursday — Half-price appetizers until 1 AM Sunday — Prime rib dinner from 3 PM to 9 PM. Upstairs at the Earl has live bands Thursday and Saturday nights and karaoke on the Friday. Downstairs its ladies night Wednesdays featuring an acoustic guitarist. Sunday the upstairs has different theme nights, please call for details.

The Emerald Isle

Address: 6298 Main Street, Stouffville
Telephone: 905-642-2122
Proprietor: Pauline Ashmore
Opened: 2001
Bar: 9 Draft Taps

A little piece of Ireland in Stouffville with Dublin lass Pauline at the helm of this traditional pub. The sit-down bar is to the left and the dining area to the right, with tables and chairs in an elevated section at the back. The front windows open up to a small streetside patio that stays open until 11 PM. All sports teams receive complimentary finger foods. The menu has many traditional Irish dishes and a great pizza selection. Wednesday the ribs are on special and Thursday is pasta night. An Irish breakfast is available on Saturdays and Sundays from 9 AM and homemade gourmet burgers are the special on Sunday night. Entertainment is an electric jam every Thursday with house band the "Black Velvet Scrunchie." Friday and Saturday nights have live Celtic music.

❖

The Lion of Stouffville

Address: 5917 Main Street, Stouffville
Telephone: 905-642-1344
Proprietor: Graham Hoad
Opened: 1999
Bar: 20 Draft Taps.

The long sit-down bar stretches to the right as you enter the pub where you will find several booths and a large darts area. The main dining section is a mixture of booths and bench seating. The enclosed patio out front has many shrubs and flowering plants giving a beautiful garden backdrop to summer days. The bar was the winner of the Stouffville Sun readers' choice award for all-round best restaurant and patio in 2000. The food at the Lion is well known for its high quality as Graham, himself a qualified chef, makes sure that nothing but the best goes into his menu. The daily specials are excellent, especially the very popular catch of the day. The menu features a very varied selection, including traditional fare. A good selection of wines and scotches is available to complement any meal. Entertainment in summer months consists of a live band on the patio every Thursday evening.

The Scarlet Gryffyn

Address: 107 Erie Street, Stratford
Telephone: 519-273-3666/**Web:** http://www.stratfordhotel.on.ca
Innkeeper: David Mullock
Opened: 1997
Bar: 8 Draft Taps

Housed in the Stratford Hotel, which was built in 1875, this elegant Victorian-style pub and dining room is a luxurious step back in time. The large dining area has a large aquarium at one end of the room and this adds a touch of serenity to the luxury. Stratford is home to the annual Stratford Festival of theatre from April 25th to November 4th and various props from the festival theatre adorning this large bar are in keeping with the Victorian theme. There is an area for darts by the bar and downstairs is the Beefeater sports bar complete with big screen, pool tables and off track betting. The menu has a fantastic selection of AAA steaks including filet mignon and a large 24-oz Porterhouse to name but a few. Seafood is also a part of the dining experience and includes lobster, oysters, shrimp and salmon. An afternoon Devon cream tea is also served. The Stratford has 12 gorgeous rooms each with Queen-size beds and fireplaces. For something different why not catch a murder mystery at the inn and then take advantage of a special package deal and stay the night.

❖

Bentley's

Address: 99 Ontario Street, Stratford
Telephone: 519-271-1121
Proprietor: Brian Bentley and Caroline Hood
Opened 1986
Bar: 17 Draft Taps

This unique-looking pub has leather-topped bar stools and a tiled floor surrounding the sit-down bar which sits elevated in the centre of the room. The rest of the bar and dining areas are surrounded by luxurious booths lining the perimeters. There are also two open dining areas. The art hanging throughout the bar can be described as a mix of mythology and Greek theatre, this is open to discussion as that is only one man's opinion. The menu is mainly North American with traditional fare and pizza selections. Bentley's is also an inn with many bi-level suites. Entertainment periodical in winter, please call for details.

Streetsville

The Cock and Pheasant

Address: 63 Queen Street, Streetsville
Telephone: 905-542-8741
Proprietor: Kate Miller
Opened: 1997
Bar: 14 Draft Taps

Look for the red British phone box by the road and that is your cue to turn into the picturesque plaza called Trinity Square where you will find this traditional British-style pub. Popular with local soccer fans the pub shows most games on the big screen. A patio wraps around the side of the pub looking out onto a green belt. The menu is mixed and includes traditional fare as well as the following evening specials: Monday — Wings; Tuesday — Fajita frenzy; Wednesday — Two-for-one curry; Thursday: Two-for-one appetizers; and Fridays — fish and chip dinner. Live bands every Saturday night.

❖

The Winchester Arms

Address: 158 Queen Street South, Streetsville
Telephone: 905-567-5936
Proprietor: Brent Ottewill
Opened: 1980
Bar: 14 Draft Taps

The dining area in this pub is off to the left and has two levels with plenty of booths. It is beautifully furnished and would not be out of place in a five-star hotel. Among the many draft beers the bar has is the in-house Winchester Gold, a premium lager at a domestic price. The bar has dartboards and two of the ever popular Golden Tee golf games. The patio looks out onto the main street and has a covered section containing a pool table. The menu is a traditional/North American mix with the following evening specials: Monday — Fish and chips; Tuesday and Wednesday — Wings; Thursday — Full rack of ribs; Friday and Saturday: Prime rib dinner and Sunday kids eat free (one child per adult). Entertainment is periodical so please call for details.

Sudbury

Grumblers English Pub

Address: 1620 Regent Street South, Sudbury
Telephone: 705-522-2700
Proprietor: Don
Opened: 1995
Bar: 17 Draft Taps

A traditional English-style pub and the most northern one in this guide. The interior is a mix of brick and wallpaper with an old-fashioned ceiling. The walls have plenty of pub memorabilia including carvings purchased in England. A pool table and dartboards are also in the bar area while a sports bar is downstairs complete with off track betting. A full menu with a good mixed selection and many daily specials. Sunday, Monday, and Tuesday are wing nights and the recommended prime rib roast is every Friday and Saturday evening. Entertainment is provided by a disc jockey Thursday, Friday and Saturdays.

❖

Carriages

Address: 27 Bridge Street East, Thornbury
Telephone: 519-599-2217
Proprietors: Rob and Anne Wildman
Opened: 1988
Bar: 4 Draft Taps

The first Reeve of Thornbury built this large manse as his home way back in 1860. Now it's an elegant country inn with a cozy English pub on the main floor. The inn is right next to Thornbury's dam and fish ladder and it is indeed a marvelous sight to witness the salmon overcoming this hurdle on their way upstream. The patio at the rear of the pub overlooks a mill pond on the property and also adds an air of serenity to your visit. The inn features fine dining and also four luxurious guest rooms. Very popular in both summer and winter with tourists, as Thornbury sits right on the scenic Georgian Triangle. The pub is a great place to meet people from all countries at the small sit-down bar, and you will find Rob and Anne very hospitable hosts

Piper's Restaurant & Tavern

Address: 54 King Street East, Thornbury
Telephone: 519-599-1888
Proprietor: Joe MacDonald
Opened: 2001
Bar: 18 Draft Taps.

The picturesque town of Thornbury lies just west of Collingwood along the shores of Georgian Bay and here you will find a little piece of Scotland in the shape of the Piper. You don't have to look far to see the kilt here as they are hanging on every wall. The patio out back looks out over a mature wooded area. A downstairs room is available for private parties. The menu is mostly homemade with a large traditional section and excellent daily specials. Customers have to sign a release diploma form when ordering wings with the "ladies from hell" fire sauce and when finished the diploma goes up on the wall with the other brave souls. A busy open jam session every Tuesday and live bands every weekend.

Allen's

Address: 143 Danforth Avenue, Toronto
Telephone: 416-463-3086
Proprietor: John Maxwell
Opened: 1987
Bar: 16 Draft Taps

Extensive use of wood, a tin ceiling and an oak plank floor along with a grand oak sit-down bar that dominates the front room is John Maxwell's tribute to the Irish-American saloons of his native New York. The award-winning backyard patio is watched over by three 100-year-old willow trees and is a busy lunch spot in the summer. The bar has Toronto's most extensive beer list with over 90 from all over the world, and the single malt selection is not too shabby either with over 130 brands. A varied menu with an array of Irish traditional dishes and many daily specials. Tuesday and Saturday nights feature live Celtic music.

The Artful Dodger

Address: 10 Isabella Street, Toronto
Telephone: 416-964-9511
General Manager: Tom
Opened: 1979
Bar: 14 Draft Taps

Named after the streetwise pick-pocket from Oliver Twist, this Victorian-style manse has a dining room to the left as you step through the front door and a small seating area and sit-down bar to the right. Upstairs has a pool table and dartboards during the winter months with summer seeing the pool table moved to the back patio where an outside bar is open nightly. The upstairs is then used as a function room. A North American menu with a traditional pub fare section including the following evening specials: Monday — Burgers; Tuesday — Pizza; Wednesday — All-day ribs, wings and fries; Thursday — Wings; Saturday: Steak and Sunday a prime rib dinner. A weekend brunch is available from 11 AM to 4 PM. Every Monday is trivia night.

❖

The Auld Spot Pub

Address: 347 Danforth Avenue, Toronto
Telephone: 416-406-4688
Proprietor: Herb Bradley
Opened: 1998
Bar: 13 Draft Taps

This small Danforth pub has a cozy interior with a Scottish back-drop. A small sit-down bar is a good place to start. Try one of the many single malts before you sit down at a table to order from the menu, which features traditional gourmet Scottish foods among which the smoked salmon is considered delicious. On the other hand you can try the deep-fried Mars bar and chips. The pub specials steer away from the traditional with Wednesday being "discover a new curry" night; other specials include half-price mussels on Mondays, and Sunday it's back to tradition with a fabulous roast beef dinner. A substantial wine list is available to suit any palate. The Auld Spot puts on a great Burns' Night which is booked well in advance.

The Bishop and the Belcher

Address: 361 Queen Street, Toronto
Telephone: 416-591-2352
Proprietors: Jennifer and Anita
Opened: 1995
Bar: 16 Draft taps

This very English-style pub has pool tables and dartboards in the back dining area which leads out to the courtyard patio. Plenty of beer on tap, including a couple of local micro breweries. An international menu also includes many traditional selections. The management recommend the in-house specialty, the Big Belch, which is a combination of wings and other appetizers that are not for the timid. Evening specials are as follows: Sunday — Jumbo wings; Monday — International night featuring Mexican, Greek, Thai and Indian cuisine; Tuesday — Pasta; and Wednesday has the steak dinner.

The Black Bull

Address: 298 Queen Street West, Toronto
Telephone: 416-593-2766
Proprietor: Bobby Taylor
Opened: 1973
Bar: 13 Draft Taps

Situated in a large red brick heritage building dating back to 1833, the Bull takes up the corner of Queen and Soho. The side patio is the largest on Queen and draws a big summer-time crowd. The pub has been written up in many historical building guides and there has been a tavern on this site for over a hundred years. A big-screen TV and pool table are in the front of the bar as you walk in. During the day the Bull attracts customers from the surrounding businesses and at night the pub consists of the many types who call the downtown core home. The full menu includes traditional and Canadian pub fare. Entertainment starts in the fall and consists of live bands on Friday and Saturdays.

Black Dog Pub

Address: 87 Island Road, West Rouge, Toronto
Telephone: 416-286-4544
Proprietor: Ken Rueter
Opened: 1993
Bar: 21 Draft Taps

The original Black Dog pub consisted of only one thousand square feet and six employees; because the place was so small and business booming Ken invested in a state-of-the-art air system for the comfort of his customers and staff. The pub had gained in popularity so much that another sixteen hundred feet was added, including a smoke-free stately dining room and a beautiful floral garden. A cigar room also added was later changed to a party/banquet room. The Black Dog has since upgraded its air system to one of the finest and most mimicked in the restaurant business. The pub has won in the past over nine awards from various organizations for best pub, and as the word is spreading the pub now employs over 50 people. A large selection of single malts and a good wine list is available along with many micro brews on tap. The menu is an international selection containing many pub favourites as well as a good heart smart section.

❖

The Black Sheep

Address: 4901 Yonge Street, Toronto
Telephone: 416-224-0741
Proprietor: Sammy
Opened: 1983
Bar: 13 Draft Taps

One of the most well-known British-style pubs in Toronto the Black Sheep has long been a favourite watering hole for exiles. A large area at the back has dartboards and three booths lining the wall while the bar area has two large bench booths that are perfect for larger groups. The pub added an adjoining games room a few years back with pool tables, video games and two large screens. This room is available for private functions and has an overhead garage door entrance that opens up to the street in summer. A varied menu with wing specials every night. Karaoke at the pub every Saturday night.

The Bow and Arrow

Address: 1954 Yonge Street, Toronto
Telephone: 416-487-2036
Proprietor: Keiron Meaney
Opened: 1992
Bar: 23 Draft Taps

Part of the Arrow Group, which believes in using and promoting local merchants and breweries. The draft selection contains local micro breweries and cask-conditioned ales. Upstairs is available for private functions and is also the home of the Central Toronto Glasgow Rangers supporters club. The downstairs bar has a dart room in the back and the windows at the front open on to the street. The bar has an excellent selection of single malts and periodically hosts mini festivals featuring a local brewery. In the fall there is a week-long festival that marries beer and foods and features many local micro breweries and produce. The menu has a great selection of burgers and thin-crust pizza and there are daily specials featuring both. Entertainment every Sunday between September and June features one of the best East coast bands, Sandy McIntyre and Family.

Bryden's Red Lion

Address: 449 Jarvis Street, Toronto
Telephone: 416-967-5551
Proprietor: Bryden Tait
Opened: 2001
Bar: 11 Draft Taps

Antique couches and chairs abound in this 1891 building to give the bar an authentic Victorian parlour feel. A natural functional fireplace adds to the reality of yesteryear. A large mature patio fronts this historical house which for as long as anyone can remember has been a licensed premises. The menu ranges from Korean beef salad and curry stir fry to traditional dishes. The blackboard shows weekly dinner specials and there is a weekend brunch menu available from 10 AM until 4 PM. An excellent wine selection. Entertainment periodical, please call for details.

The Bull and Firkin

Address: 1835 Yonge Street, Toronto
Telephone: 416-485-2290
Proprietor: John Ortega
Opened: 2000
Bar: 16 Draft Taps

A long sit-down bar leads to an upper section with pool tables and a 20-foot bench with small individual tables lined up along the front of it. A separate dart area makes it perfect for teams. The lower bar area has plenty of large comfortable booths and wrought iron railings are consistent throughout the pub. The menu is a good mixture of pub fare, sandwiches and steaks. Wings are the most popular food here and they are on special all day Saturday and Sunday, Monday from 4 PM to 11 PM and Tuesday to Friday from 4 PM to 7 PM. N.T.N. trivia at the bar

C'est What?

Address: 67 Front Street East, Toronto
Telephone: 416-867-9499
Proprietors: Brenda Atkinson and George Milbrandt
Opened: 1988
Bar: 20 Draft Taps

True local flavour is served here. This cozy, funky hang–out show-cases the diverse and vibrant city of Toronto. A great value menu of multicultural comfort food is served all open hours. Favourites such as lamburger, falafel, chicken satay, lemongrass noodles, porter beef ribs, and steak and frites are priced from $7 to $12. Five home-brewed ales are served alongside two dozen other local craft beers. C'est What's adjoining lounge and live music room, "nia," is Toronto's finest small venue performance atmosphere, fea-turing fresh original pop music with an edge from local indie artists. Some notable alumni include Jewel, The Tea Party, Barenaked Ladies, Jeff Buckley, Rufus Wainwright, Roger Hodgson, Ron Sexsmith, Sarah Harmer and Hawksley Workman.

Cassidy's
Address: 2856 Danforth Avenue, Toronto
Telephone: 416-699-3564
Proprietor: John Orr
Opened: 1996
Bar: 12 Draft Taps

A traditional pub on the upper Danforth, Cassidy's is the place to be for all the Gaelic games, especially the football. Upcoming televised games are posted in the pub on Tuesdays. The bar area has a pool table and dartboards along with a juke box. A downstairs bar with seating for 50 is available for private functions. A traditional menu with many of the selections homemade, including the very popular meat pies. Wednesday is wing night. Live music every Friday and Saturday, with Sunday nights hosting the busy open mike sessions

The Court Jester
Address: 609 Danforth Avenue, Toronto
Telephone: 416-465-3700
Proprietors: Lawrie and Steve
Opened: 1996
Bar: 16 Draft Taps

Lots of mirrors line the one wall of this narrow bar and give the place a much larger feel. In summer the small sidewalk patio proves to be very popular to take in the sights and the sounds of the Danforth. This bar prides itself on its exceptional food quality, voted best food recently by Now magazine; most items are prepared fresh daily by chef Steve Suita. The menu has a large selection of traditional pub fare. Daily specials are as follows: Monday — Thai noodles with shrimp chicken and tofu; Tuesday — gourmet cheeseburgers; Wednesday and Sunday — wing specials; Saturday — rib and wing combo. All-day breakfast and weekend brunch.

Dora Keogh's
Address: 141 Danforth Avenue, Toronto
Telephone: 416-778-1804
Proprietor: John Maxwell
Opened: 1997
Bar: 12 Draft Taps

A very authentic country pub with bench and stool seating, a cozy snug and a large wood-burning fireplace. The bar features pressed-copper tables and weathered hardwood floors. There is a scattering of cozy booths for the more intimate pint of Guinness. An area at the back affectionately known as Yer Ma's Kitchen has to be booked a week in advance. It's for groups of eight to fourteen, who are then seated around a rustic wooden table and for a set price offered a select menu fit for a king, including roast pork with cracklin`, leg of lamb with garlic, Belfast ham, and many other succulent dishes. Entertainment on Thursdays and Sundays consists of the best local Irish musicians in internationally acclaimed sessions. Past guests have included the world famous Chieftains.

The Duke of Gloucester
Address: 649 Yonge Street, Toronto
Telephone: 416-961-9704
Proprietors: Monique and Jonathon
Opened: 1976
Bar: 18 Draft Taps

Up a flight of steps from the Yonge Street entrance, this long narrow pub has a pool table and dartboards at the back and an open sitting area at the front. The long bar has many etched glass and wooden dividers which gives the feeling of being in a smaller place and also a touch of privacy. One of the first pubs to show live soccer games, the Duke is home to many Canadian supporters' associations of major British soccer teams. The menu is a mix of traditional and North American fare with a very popular all-day British breakfast. Monday and Wednesday are wing nights. Entertainment every second Saturday, and every Friday is pub night for the many supporters groups.

❖

The Duke of Argyle

Address: 86 John Street, Toronto
Telephone: 416-340-9700
General Manager: Natalie Baker
Opened: 2001
Telephone: 15 Draft Taps

The dark woods and subtle lighting add a warmth matched only by the hospitality in this Nova Scotia–style pub. The sounds of the east coast play continuously in the background, enriching the cozy atmosphere. A large north-facing patio deck with a capacity for over one hundred people is the scene for many busy Saturday evenings featuring live Celtic music. The large dining area to the back of the bar has many booths for quieter times. A good selection of single malts on hand with over 50 stocked. The menu is a rich mix of traditional and North American fare with many excellent daily specials including a generous serving of haddock and chips, which is the most popular dish in the bar. Summertime sees lobster night every Saturday with live lobster flown in from Nova Scotia. Entertainment features live Celtic music every Friday and Saturday night.

The Duke of Kent

Address: 2315 Yonge Street, Toronto
General Manager: Mea Hill
Opened: 1976
Bar: 19 Draft Taps

A small, comfortable pub with an elevated section of booths lining the one wall. The sit-down bar to the left is always busy, as this Duke is one of the most popular spots in uptown Toronto, especially with expatriates, many of whom have been regulars from opening day. The pub has an annual picnic on Toronto Island which is always a great success. The patio is a great place to relax and watch the busy Yonge Street corridor as its traffic and people rush by. Included in the many drafts are cask-conditioned ales, and a good selection of single malts are also available. A large mixed menu with Tuesday and Thursday being an all-day curry special, while Saturday and Sunday feature all-you-can-eat mussels. Sunday is euchre day, please call for details.

The Duke of Richmond
Address: 20 Queen Street West, Toronto
Telephone: 416-340-7887
General Manager: Adam Watkinson
Opened: 1998
Bar: 20 Draft Taps

Located in the Cadillac Fairview Tower on the lower level and next to the main Yonge subway line, this Duke has a very busy cocktail hour with many commuters taking a relaxing time-out to enjoy the atmosphere of this cozy traditional British-style pub. Thirsty Thursday tastings feature samplings of draft beers with a different brand selected every week. Traditional and international fare on the menu is prepared by well-known Toronto chef Amer Mokdad and his specials are well-anticipated delights. After a busy day in Toronto before catching the subway home, pop in for a pint and a bite at this comfortable downtown pub.

❖

The Duke of Westminster

Address: 77 Adelaide Street West. Toronto
Telephone: 416-368-2761
General Manager: Ian Wood
Opened: 1977
Bar: 18 Draft Taps

Located below ground at the foot of the First Canadian Place shopping centre, the Duke has both an east and west entrance with the long narrow bar connecting both. The bar area's narrow corridor is lined with charming two-seater booths. At one end is a small dining section while at the other end is an alcove with a darts room. The décor of the whole pub is very traditional with red velvet upholstery and plush carpeting throughout; on the walls hang many English prints, with most focusing on Westminster in London. Downstairs has the Grand Hall, a large dining room that seats almost 200; the Boardroom is a private dining room available for lunchtime business meetings. In between is the stockbrokers' bar affectionately known as the Swamp, where in between pints the clientele watch the ticker. A large menu with weekly specials placed on each table features many traditional dishes, including an excellent chicken curry. The Duke is closed Saturdays and Sundays but this impressive bar is available for private hire.

❖

The Duke of York

Address: 39 Prince Arthur Avenue, Toronto
Telephone: 416-964-2441
General Manager: Kim Bartley
Opened: 1975
Bar: 20 Draft Taps

The original Duke of York pub, which was built in Southampton, England, and shipped over piece by piece, is still downstairs where over the years it has blossomed into three floors. This Victorian pub can be booked for private parties or, as in the past, weddings. The main floor has a long oak sit-down bar and two separate dining areas called the Prince Arthur Rooms which are beautifully furnished. The large backyard patio is surrounded by ivy-covered high fencing and mature trees to give a very secluded, peaceful garden effect. The Queen Bess Room upstairs is non-smoking, has cozy corner booths and a fireplace along with a Tudor bar and windowed balcony, and makes a great floor for large party groups. A traditional/North American fare menu with plenty of daily and evening specials. The pub is located one block from Varsity Stadium.

The Elephant and Castle

Address: 378 Yonge Street. Toronto
Telephone: 416-598-4003
Proprietors: Elephant and Castle Group
Opened: 1999
Bar: 18 Draft Taps

This classy bar is situated in an old bank building with high ceilings and windows and the light décor adds to its majestic air. The sit-down bar itself is almost 40 feet long and runs a third of the length of this narrow building. There is an upstairs mezzanine which is very popular at lunchtime with large office groups. There is an old service elevator still in use and the original bank vault is still intact downstairs. A good selection of single malts is available. Menu is large and mainly traditional with excellent daily specials.

The Elephant and Castle

Address: 212 King Street West. Toronto
Telephone: 416-598-4455
General Manager: Steve Meeker
Opened: 1996
Bar: 20 Draft Taps

A long sit-down bar to the left as you enter from King Street with a dining area to the right would be big enough for most bars but in the Elephant and Castle the journey is just beginning. The pub opens up to a larger section containing different theme rooms: there is the games room with three pool tables, there is the library dining room, the Simcoe room taking you back to an era in Canadian history, and the rustic cottage room. At the other end of this large pub and eatery is the Office Bar which can be rented for large private parties. The bar here is horseshoe-shaped making it perfect for interactive conversation. A patio runs the length of the pub between King and Pearl on Simcoe. An extensive menu with a large selection of traditional dishes and daily specials.

The Feathers

Address: 962 Kingston Road, Toronto
Telephone: 416-694-0443
Proprietor: Ian Innes
Opened: 1981
Bar: 21 Draft Taps

The single malt capital of Ontario, the Feathers has over three hundred varieties, including many that can only be found in Canada in this pub. Ian Innes has made the selecting and tasting of this nectar of the gods his life-long quest and along with one of his business partners makes regular treks back to Scotland to purchase quality malts for his patrons back at the bar. The walls are adorned with one-of-a-kind photos of many Scottish distilleries. The single malts are reasonably priced compared to regular market pricing and many are imported privately. Along with the whisky the Feathers has four in-house brews as well as hand-pumped real ales from Wellington Brewery. The menu is very traditional and is made fresh daily. Entertainment every Saturday night.

The Ferret and Firkin

Address: 720 Spadina Avenue, Toronto
Telephone: 416-962-2016
Proprietor: Larry Issacs
Opened: 1995
Bar: 16 Draft Taps

The long sit-down bar is needed most evenings and weekends, as this large pub sits right on the edge of campus and is very popular with students. A back area known as the Burrow opens daily at 5:30 and contains two pool tables and a separate dart area along with a jukebox. The front bar area has its own pool table and plenty of seating including booths. A large patio seats upward of 80 and has many flowering shrubs. A good mix of sandwiches, salads and pub fare make up the large menu along with many daily specials. The Ferret has martini night on Tuesday and ladies night on Wednesdays; entertainment is a disc jockey on Saturdays and karaoke on Sunday evenings.

Fiddlers Green

Address: 27 Wellesley Street, Toronto
Telephone: 416-967-9447.
Proprietors: Ian, Teresa and Paul McDonald
Opened: 1998
Bar: 16 Draft Taps

Situated in the historical Somerset House built in 1873 by James Cox Aitkins, the secretary of state under Sir John A. MacDonald, the Fiddlers is across the street from the Wellesley subway station. Walking into this century building the small bar is to the left and the dining room to the right. Upstairs houses a function room that can be booked for any occasion. The large patio has plenty of shade provided by many mature trees. A good selection of single malts. The menu is a good mix and includes regular favourites; the bar also claims to have the best fish and chips in Toronto.

Fionn MacCool's Irish Pub

Address: 70 The Esplanade, Toronto
Telephone: 416-362-2495
General Manager: Glenn Miller
Opened: 1997
Bar: 20 Draft Taps

Located in the heart of downtown Toronto, Fionn MacCool's is a prime spot for gathering for both business and social events. The pub has four main areas including the common area, the bar, the snug and the patio. The staff are very friendly and dressed in traditional attire and welcome customers as they enter this unique Irish bar. A good selection of single malts and fine Irish whiskies along with a fully stocked humidor. Authentic Irish fare is prepared by Fionn MacCool's own chef and her crew daily and an all-day brunch menu is offered at weekends. The best in live Celtic and east coast music weekly from Wednesday through Saturday.

The Flatiron and Firkin

Address: 49 Wellington Street East, Toronto
Telephone: 416-362-3444
Proprietors: Susanne MacLeod
Opened: 2000
Bar: 11 Draft Taps

Located on the ground floor of the famous Flatiron Building which has been the backdrop for countless movies and commercials. The entrance to the bar is the tip of the iron-shaped building and as you walk through the room gets wider and wider, hence the flatiron name. A large patio on the south side is fast becoming one of the busiest in the city, along with its unique backdrop and central location. The bar is below street level with the upper windows looking onto the street above, jammed open by actual vintage flatirons. The menu is North American fare with a great selection of steaks from the grill. The wings are on special daily except for Thursday and Friday and an excellent curry is on special Tuesday and Thursday. Entertainment on special occasions, please call for details.

Fox and Fiddle

Address: 190 Laird Drive, Toronto
Telephone: 416-467-8682
General Manager: Art Giewleski
Opened: 1999
Bar: 23 Draft Taps

A large open bar with two large areas separated by brick arches and a central fireplace. Large metal circular chandeliers hang from the ceiling between thick wooden beams, looking like something you would find in a medieval banquet hall. One section has two pool tables and five large booths while the bar area has a large pull-down projection screen. N.T.N. trivia is available at the bar. The menu contains a good cross-section with an excellent array of sandwiches. Monday to Friday from 4 PM to 6 PM the bar features half-price appetizers, Sunday and Monday is create-your-own-pasta night, Wednesday is half-price fajitas and Friday and Saturday the popular prime rib dinner. Entertainment is periodical so please call for details.

❖

Fox and Fiddle

Address: 106 John Street, Toronto
Telephone: 416-593-4407
General Manager: George Zakas
Opened: 2001
Bar: 20 Draft Taps

Formerly a students' dormitory, this one-hundred-year-old building now houses the Fox and Fiddle and they have kept the charm both on the outside and interior of this beautiful heritage manse. The downstairs bar has polished wooden floors and an oak sit-down bar while in an alcove to one side is a cozy little dining area with traditional carpeting. Upstairs is a charming room with an oak bar with a blue marble top and the same polished wooden floors. There is a gas fireplace at the far end of the room and a central stand-up bar while a small rooftop patio looks out onto the Toronto skyline. The menu is a traditional/North American mix with many daily specials. Entertainment every Thursday, Friday and Saturday evenings may feature a disc jockey or live music.

The Fox and Firkin

Address: 51 Eglinton Avenue East, Toronto
Telephone: 416-480-0200
Proprietor: Ian Fisher
Opened: 1986
Bar: 16 Draft Taps

The first of the Firkins, this popular Yonge and Eglinton bar still packs them in, although the area has seen the amount of pubs and clubs double in the past few years. A large backyard patio with the presence of mature trees offers plenty of shade on sunny days. Darts are available as well as the N.T.N. trivia game. Every day has wing specials and there is a weekend brunch from 11:30 AM until 3 PM. Menu is a good cross-section with daily pasta, pie and catch of the day specials. Karaoke on every first and third Sunday of the month.

The Foxes Den

Address: 1075 Bay Street, Toronto
Telephone: 416-961-1975
Proprietor: Michael Chan
Opened: 1996
Bar: 13 Draft Taps

An upper section at the rear of the pub has two pool tables and dartboards. A large-screen TV shows all major soccer games. A patio at the front of the bar and one at the side offers the choice of sun or shade. A good selection of wines to complement the large menu which includes oven-baked pizza and an excellent south-western grill section. Evening specials are as follows: Monday — Wings; Tuesday — Super-sized nachos; Wednesday — Burgers; and on Sundays all of the preceding specials are available. Sunday also sees a brunch from 11 AM to 3 PM. Proud of the fact that all of the staff have been there from day one.

The Friar and Firkin
Address: 160 John Street, Toronto
Telephone: 416-340-9459
General Manager: Paul Sariva
Opened: 1990
Bar: 16 Draft Taps

Situated on the busy corner of John and Queen, this cozy pub is a few steps down from street level and features an elevated back section with comfortable booth seating. The popular patio sits on John and with seating for only 26 it fills up quickly. The bar has a busy after-work crowd who like the comfort and quiet atmosphere of this traditional pub. Only steps away from the City TV and Muchmusic building, it is not unusual to see local celebrities enjoying a quiet pint in the Friar. The menu features many traditional and regular fare dishes and also excellent daily specials; the grilled swordfish is exceptional.

The Frog and Firkin
Address: 4854 Yonge Street, Toronto
Telephone: 416225-3764
General Manager: Paul Sariva
Opened: 1994
Bar: 16 Draft Taps

Originally the well-known Victoria and Albert, the Frog took over seven years ago, keeping all the faithful regulars and adding many more with their friendly neighbourhood approach. The pub is horseshoe-shaped with the bar at the top end and comfortable booths lining both areas leading up to the bar. Ask for the Firkin brew which is a few ounces more than a pint but for the same price. A big-screen TV behind the bar is perfect for the sports fans seated there. Upstairs has three pool tables, dartboards and a capacity for two hundred. There is also a large room available for private functions. A mixed menu with a variety of daily lunch specials and the popular wings which are specially priced throughout the week, ask your server for details. When in the pub ask for Olive who has been there from day one and is well known for her friendliness and dry Scottish humour.

The Hargrave

Address: 1106 Danforth Avenue, Toronto
Telephone: 416-465-4500
Proprietor: Chris Wood
Opened: 1999 (under present management)
Bar: 10 Draft Taps

The front windows of this English-style traditional pub slide open to allow access to the patio and street. At the rear of the pub is a pool table and dartboards and on Mondays the pool is free after 3 PM. N.T.N. trivia is available at the bar along with a good selection of single malts. Menu is a mix of traditional and North American fare with a section of Texmex specials. Wednesday is half-price wings from 5 PM to close. Sunday special is a popular prime rib dinner with a weekend brunch also available from 11 AM until 3 PM.

Hemingway's

Address: 142 Cumberland Street, Toronto
Telephone: 416-968-2828
Proprietor: Martin McSkimming
Opened: 1980
Bar: 16 Draft Taps

Named after the famed writer, photographs of Papa line the downstairs wall. The interior of the bar is green including the table tops and carpet. A large-screen TV at the far end is cleverly set into the wall. The bar has a small street-side patio as well as a very popular rooftop patio which is heated and has its own full-service bar and a large covered section. Also upstairs is a separate pool room. Hemingway's has an excellent wine list and a dinner menu that ranges from fajitas to curried lamb; there is also a section containing traditional fare. Entertainment on a regular basis, please call for details.

Irish Embassy
Address: 49 Yonge Street, Toronto
Telephone: 416-866-8282
Proprietors: Rory and Gavin
Opened: 2001
Bar: 16 Draft Taps

This upscale pub and grill is located on the corner of Yonge and Wellington in an old heritage building that was once home to a bank in the 1870s. The grandeur of the place is the first thing to hit when you enter the Embassy with its 40-foot high ceiling and four massive marble support pillars. Less than a year open, the place has already become a favourite spot for the local Bay Street crowd and tourists alike. The décor is in keeping with the feeling of a bygone splendour and the seating is comfortable from the booths to the barstools. Three menus are available, for lunch, dinner and snacks, and all feature a good selection including traditional Irish fare, seafood and sandwiches. A favourite for the health-conscious meat lover is the bison burger. So when you are looking for a visa to drink Guinness or Smithwicks, go no further than the Irish Embassy.

The James Joyce
Address: 386 Bloor Street West, Toronto
Telephone: 416-324-9400
General Manager: Ross Kelly
Opened: 1993
Bar: 12 Draft Taps

Named after one of Ireland's greatest writers, this corner pub has a large back section with two pool tables and a large-screen TV for all the big soccer games and sporting events. Among the draft selection are two house brands, the James Joyce red and the gold lager. A mixed menu with a good selection of hearty Irish fare. The wings are on special every day and on the colder nights why not try the black beer chili. Entertainment is provided every night of the week, consisting mostly of Irish bands.

The Jersey Giant

Address: 71 Front Street, Toronto
Telephone: 416-368-4095
Proprietor: Joan Zarry
Opened: 1986
Bar: 16 Draft Taps

This Tudor-décor pub with its large wooden beams criss crossing the high ceiling is a welcome relief from the busy Front Street crowds. A small central bar is the focal point of the room and there is a dining room section at street level where the window slides open to a small patio on the street. A narrow hallway lined with tables leads to the games room at the back with pool tables, dartboards and a golf machine. A jukebox is also available. A large mixed menu with the following evening specials: Monday — Wings and 15% off for fellow industry workers; Tuesday — Pasta; Wednesday — Burgers; Thursday — Souvlaki; Friday — Open-faced turkey dinner, and Monday to Friday between 4 PM and 6 PM free appetizers with purchase of beverage.

The King's Arms

Address: 158 Cumberland Street, Toronto
Telephone: 416-935-0405
Proprietor: Randy Petrie
Opened: 2001
Bar: 15 Draft Taps

Two-level pub with the upstairs available for private parties and functions. The small bar downstairs has a cozy atmosphere and due to the proximity to the Four Seasons Hotel it is not unusual to see a few famous faces there during the Toronto Film Festival. The menu is popular pub fare with four daily specials and for groups the staff recommend the large hot plate special. In the summer months the small street-side patio has Saturday afternoon entertainment. Upstairs has entertainment Wednesday, Thursday and Saturday nights.

Kitty O'Shea's

Address: 2375 Queen Street East, Toronto
Telephone: 416-690-7827
Proprietor: Robert Costelloe
Opened: 2000
Bar: 10 Draft Taps

This small piece of Ireland in the Beaches area of Toronto is possibly the smallest pub in Canada and certainly in Ontario with a capacity of 26 (the Wee Jaggy Nettle is licensed for 25 but has an additional 30 on the patio). What it lacks in space it makes up for in character and atmosphere; also the home of the Toronto Beaches Celtic supporters club. The bar shows Scottish premier soccer live every weekend and covers all major soccer events as well as the six nations rugby. The windows slide open in summer to allow the capacity to swell to 28 if you count the two guys sitting on the window sill. A gas fireplace sits in the centre of this little pub and there is also a dartboard. The menu is bar snacks only. Entertainment is on the 15th and 30th of each month.

The Lion on the Beach

Address: 1958 Queen Street East, Toronto
Telephone: 416-690-1984
Proprietor: Bruce
Opened: 1990
Bar: 16 Draft Taps

A favourite Beaches watering hole for the past decade, the Lion has a large wrap-around patio which offers the greatest vantage point to watch the colourful mix of locals and tourists passing by. A friendly game of darts is always available, with many of the regulars up for the challenge. The menu is a traditional/North American mix. All-day breakfast and a late evening snack menu is available along with the following nightly specials: Monday — Steak; Tuesday — Half-price wings; Wednesday — Prime rib; Thursday — Ribs; and Friday is the Thai noodle. An excellent brunch menu every Saturday and Sunday. Entertainment is every Saturday and Sunday evening.

❖

Mad Monty's Pub
Address: 2655 Yonge Street, Toronto
Telephone: 416-488-3976
Proprietor: Douglas Montgomery
Opened: 19
Bar: 8 Draft Taps

This charming uptown neighbourhood pub is well known for its friendliness and homemade lunch specials. A recently renovated patio now has more seating for the Yonge Street sun worshippers. A second floor to the pub has a full-service bar, fireplace and big screen and can be booked free of charge for private functions. The menu is a mixture of sandwiches and homemade pub fare with the following evening specials: Monday — Half-price wings; Tuesday and Wednesday — Wing and Draft night; Thursday — Texas ribs and fries; Friday — Fish and chips. The Texas ribs are truly Texan in size. Entertainment every Thursday night, please call for details.

McMurphy's
Address: 381 Eglinton Avenue East, Toronto
Telephone: 416-489-1111
Proprietor: Neilus Mc Donald
Opened: 1990
Bar: 9 Draft Taps

This friendly Irish neighbourhood pub draws from the large number of apartments in the area and also the local Irish community. A sit-down bar is to the left and a small seating area to the right with the bands playing at the rear of this little pub, which is always busy at the weekends. The menu is a small mix of pub fare, not a large selection but value for money. Entertainment weekly and the regulars will tell you that McMurphy's has the best all-day St. Patrick's party around.

Madison Avenue Pubs and Restaurant
Address: 14-16 Madison Avenue, Toronto
Telephone: 416-961-0570
Proprietors: Dave and Isabel Manore
Opened: 1983
Bar: 22 Draft Taps

The Madison has ten bars and five patios with over 22 different beers flowing through 137 taps. The pub has to be the rooftop patio party central of Toronto, with a large cabana bar that is heated all the way around to ensure maximum year-round enjoyment. Different-level decks reveal more patio bars and plenty of seating. The Mad. bar features an old piano and many booths and also a gas fireplace and small snug. The bar has an overhead garage door that opens up to the patio. The piano bar features a baby grand and has entertainment Thursday, Friday and Saturday evenings. The Boardroom has dartboards, plenty of booths and a stand-up bar. Balls I has large banquet tables, making it perfect for larger groups; it also contains a large-screen TV, two pool tables and two fireplaces. Balls II has two large screens and occasional entertainment. Another bar called the Party Room has plenty of booths. There are also a few smaller quieter bars and each bar area has its own washroom facilities. To keep this pub going in beer the two coolers hold a total of 210 kegs. The menu is great cross-section with many lunch and evening specials. The Madison also has a hotel next door with 22 suites and there is also a sister luxury resort in Puerta Vallarta, Mexico; ask Dave and Isabel for details. The Madison Pub has to be experienced.

❖

McVeigh's

The corner of Church and Richmond, Toronto
Telephone: 416-364-9698
Proprietor: Jimmy McVeigh
Opened: 1961
Bar: 12 Draft Taps

For over 40 years this Irish-owned bar has been serving the best in food and beverage to Torontonians and ex-pats alike. This place has a large part in local Irish and Scottish folklore, as for many who came over in the 60s and early 70s it was the only place that reminded them of the pubs back home. Today you will still find accents from all over the British Isles; many are tourists but most are regulars, many loyal from day one. The bar has a good selection of Scotch and Irish whiskies. The menu with mainly traditional dishes changes daily and is featured on a large blackboard. The upstairs can be booked for private parties. Entertainment six nights a week features the best in Celtic entertainment.

Mick E. Fynn's

Address: 45 Carlton Street, Toronto
Telephone: 416-598-0537
Proprietor: Stephen O'Leary
Opened: 2001
Bar: 19 Draft Taps

A well-known Toronto pub, Mick E. Fynn's moved from its original location to larger premises across from Maple Leaf Gardens. The bar has a reclaimed brick interior and is a large open area with a games section containing three pool tables and a gas fireplace. A private room is available for functions. An open kitchen with a large grill and a menu with many homemade items and a pub favourite, Guinness-battered fish and chips. Chicken wings are on special all the time. Thursday nights are pub nights with many specials and entertainment featuring a disc jockey.

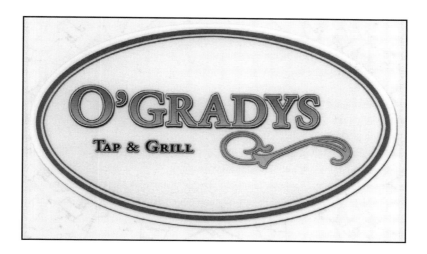

O'Grady's

Address: 171 College Street, Toronto
Telephone: 416-596-0327
General Manager: Jimmy Georgoulis
Opened: 1999
Bar: 19 Draft Tap

Located across from the University of Toronto campus, this pub serves both a neighbourhood clientele and students galore when school is in. The main room with the long sit-down bar to the left is not unlike a German beer hall with plenty of tables in the large open area. Upstairs has pool tables and dartboards and at the weekends between 5 PM and 10 PM the pool is free. A small patio sits on College. The menu is mostly North American pub fare with the following nightly specials: Monday and Sunday — Wings; Tuesday — Two-for-one pasta; Wednesday — Martinis and Fajitas; and also on Saturdays and Sundays a brunch from 10 AM until 3 PM. Thursday night is local hospital pub night, every Friday is U. OF T. pub night with disc jockey and Saturday evenings feature karaoke.

The Old Nick

Address: 123 Danforth Avenue, Toronto
Telephone: 416-461-5546
Manager: Simon Bennett
Opened: 1994
Bar: 10 Draft Taps.

This pub close to the subway line has a brick interior with a few booths here and there throughout. At the rear of the pub are dartboards and out back is a small courtyard patio. The bar has an open kitchen where you can see your meal being prepared. The menu is mixed, with a lot of pasta choices. Specials run from 3 PM until 8 PM and are as follows: Monday — Perogies; Tuesday — Nachos; Wednesday — Burgers; Thursday — Pizza; and Friday it's pasta. Brunch on Saturday and Sunday until 4 PM. Entertainment is periodical, please call for details.

P.J. O'Brien's

Address: 39 Colborne Street, Toronto
Telephone: 416-752-7562
Proprietor: John Maxwell
Opened: 1998
Bar: 10 Draft Taps

Varnished wooden floors and a copper-top bar along with a bright warm décor add to the charm of this upscale downtown bar. There are two comfortable snugs at the end of the bar and these are the popular spots for lunch and dinner. An upstairs area is available for functions and is also open in the winter for weekend entertainment. The menu is not unlike what you would find in a fine dining restaurant, with everything from Irish salmon to prime Alberta beef tenderloin, but at P.J. O'Brien's the portions are definitely larger. A good selection of single malts and fine Irish whiskies is available. A piano player entertains every Saturday night and Joe the bartender entertains every day with a story for everyone.

Paddy O'Farrell's
Address: 917 Kingston Road, Toronto
Telephone: 416-698-0880/**Web:** http://www.paddyofarrells.com
Proprietor: Patrick Farrell
Opened: 2000
Bar: 8 Draft Taps
This authentic traditional bar is like stepping back in time to the small Irish pubs of the 40s and 50s, with the walls looking like they have been made out of old door panels. The small sit-down bar makes it easy to make new friends and with a good selection of Irish whiskies on hand it does not take long at all. The menu is mainly traditional Irish pub fare, and the beef and Guinness pie has had more than a few write-ups in the local press. The anniversary of this pub is March 10th and for the whole week leading up to St. Patrick's Day the days are filled with food specials and live entertainment culminating in a fabulous Paddy's Day bash.

Pheasant and Firkin
Address: 1999 Avenue Road, North York, Toronto
Telephone: 416-483-9063
Proprietor: Claire
Opened: 1988
Bar: 16 Draft Taps
A well-established neighbourhood pub located on Avenue Road near the 401, the Pheasant was Firkin number three. When you walk in, the bar area is ahead and a hallway leads to the dining area with its many booths and cozy fireplace. A nice garden patio takes you away from the busy streets where you can watch the world rush by. Plenty of TVs play continuous sports and NTN trivia is available at the bar. A large varied menu with daily specials, and the wings are on special from 3 PM daily, ask your server for details, as some days the special lasts later than others.

Phoenix and Firkin
Address: 2175 Shepherd Avenue East, North York, Toronto
Telephone: 416-499-0383
Proprietor: Billy Lehman
Bar: 16 Draft Taps
Conveniently located next to the 401 and 404, the Phoenix also has the Shepherd bus stop right at the door. The pub is made up of three sections, including a bar area and a dining area. The back section contains two rooms, both with a pool table; one of the rooms can be booked at no charge for private functions. The bar shows all major boxing events with no cover charge on the big screen. The full menu is complemented by many daily specials, and Saturdays, Sundays, and Mondays feature wing specials. Entertainment is the best of Toronto's pub singers every Friday and Saturday evening.

Quail and Firkin
Address: 1055 Yonge Street, Toronto
Telephone: 416-962-0782
Proprietor: Marion Curtis
Opened: 1998
Bar: 16 Draft Taps
Located in the Summerhill district of Toronto, the Quail is an English-style neighbourhood pub. The bar is to the left as you walk in and there is a row of booths up the middle with the dining area to the right. A couple of steps up at the rear you will find the pool tables, dartboards and a jukebox. At the front of the bar are two Golden Tee golf games which are so popular that the bar holds a tournament every Sunday night and gives away a $50 gift certificate to the winner. The sidewalk patio sits right on Yonge Street and catches the sun most of the day. The varied menu is complemented by a variety of daily specials and the wings are on special Monday to Friday after 4 PM and all day Saturday and Sunday.

The Rose and Crown

Address: 2335 Yonge Street, Toronto
Telephone: 416-488-5557/**Web:** www.roseandcrown.com
Proprietor: Roger Best
Opened: 1979
Bar: 24 Draft Taps

Large wooden beams line the ceiling of this Tudor-style pub. Darts are popular in the Rose and Crown, with many boards lining the back wall and also a separate darts room. A back upper-level lounge is a favourite with couples as it is candlelit and furnished with comfortable love seats and sofas. In the summer the windows open up to the Yonge Street patio. The menu is a traditional/North American mix with the following evening specials: Monday — Wings; Tuesday — Pasta; Wednesday — Texmex; Thursday — Bangkok night; Friday and Saturday: Wings and nachos with pitcher special.

The Sailor's Dickey

Address: 3391 Yonge Street, Toronto
Telephone: 416-486-9311
Proprietor: Joe Kelly
Opened: 1989
Bar: 15 Draft Taps

Low black beams and red velvet upholstery give this bar a nice cozy atmosphere along with the warm orange glow from the antique-look lanterns. As the name suggests, this pub has a sea-faring look with nautical memorabilia adorning the walls. A darts area at the back, where you will also find a jukebox. A small patio facing west sits on Yonge Street allowing for maximum afternoon sun. The menu has a good variety with many lunch and dinner specials. Nachos are on special Monday nights and wings are featured on Tuesdays. Saturday and Sunday brunch is from 11 AM to 3 PM and later on the Sunday, a hearty prime rib dinner.

Scallywags
Address: 11 St. Clair Avenue, Toronto
Telephone: 416-922-3737
Proprietor: Jeff May
Opened: 1997
Bar: 17 Draft Taps

The headquarters of the Toronto Manchester United Supporters Club and when there is a game on it has quite the atmosphere. This bar has three levels, a second story which is non-smoking and then there is the heated roof-top patio and bar, a popular lunchtime spot with local businesses. The bar is big into soccer and rugby and shows all major games. Dinner menu is a cross-section of grills and pastas and there is a separate munchies menu including pizza. A large brunch is available Saturday, Sunday and holidays. Entertainment on Monday nights.

Scotland Yard
Address: 56 The Esplanade, Toronto
Telephone: 416-564-6572
Proprietor: Peter Hnatiw
Opened: 1977
Bar: 14 Draft Taps

One of Toronto's oldest and established British-style pubs, with a central sit-down bar where people like to converse after work and have a beer before the commute home. A section of the bar is a quiet little lounge known as the Library and it is here that the Toronto pub quiz league meets regularly. A pool table and dartboards are also available along with N.T.N. trivia. Original brick pillars are interspersed throughout this one-hundred-year-old building. The menu is a traditional/North American mix with the following evening specials: Monday — Chili; Tuesday — Nachos; Wednesday — Wings; Thursday — Chicken fingers; Friday — Burgers; and brunch is available Saturday and Sunday from 11:30 AM to 2:30 PM.

Scruffy Murphy's

Address: 150 Eglinton Avenue East, Toronto
Telephone: 416-231-9411/**E-mail:** scruffys@platinum1.com
General Manager: Tony Byrne
Opened: 1996
Bar: 16 Draft Taps

A large open-concept pub with a small cozy snug near the bar complete with a flickering "electric" fireplace. Big-screen TV for all sports, especially the N.F.L. on Sunday afternoons. A good selection of single malts as well as a good choice of wines. The menu has traditional Irish fare plus a lot more, including the Maharaja's chicken vindaloo, which is not for the squeamish. Saturday and Sunday brunch, with wing specials on Mondays and Tuesdays. Entertainment every Friday and Saturday with Celtic sessions on Wednesday nights. This bar frequently books well-known traditional acts from Scotland and Ireland.

❖

The Slug and Lettuce

Address: 5650 Yonge Street, Toronto
Telephone: 416-733-9690
Proprietor: Sylvia Warriner
Opened: 1990
Bar: 10 Draft Taps

Located at the busy intersection of Yonge and Finch, this bar has a long south-facing patio which catches the sun all day. A horseshoe-shaped sit-down bar makes for inclusion in friendly conversation. A popular upstairs section known as the Loft allows for a great view of the bar downstairs. High ceilings and windows make this bar seem a lot larger. A large antique clock hangs from one wall while a large-screen TV sits at the end of the dining area. A varied menu with pub favourites, and an excellent curry which changes daily, and then there is the house specialty, a delicious homemade shepherd's pie. A daily menu sheet is placed on every table. Lunchtimes are very busy in this uptown pub but the wait is well worth it.

The Spotted Dick

Address: 81 Bloor Street East, Toronto
Telephone: 416-927-0843
Proprietor: Paul Goldstein
Opened: 1984
Bar: 13 Draft Taps

Take a few steps down below street level to the well-known Spotted Dick, which is named after a regional English delicacy. The sit-down bar to the right is at least 75 to 80 feet in length, while the opposite dining area has comfortable, traditional-style seating. A pool table sits at one end of the long pub while NTN trivia is available at the bar. The walls have many English prints and along with the décor the pub has an authentic feel to it. A menu with many traditional choices, including a late breakfast that is available from 1:30 PM to 5 PM Sunday, and Monday nights feature wing specials.

Stonecutter's Arms

Address: 284 Richmond Street East, Toronto
Telephone: 416-860-0940
Proprietor: Doug
Opened: 1992
Bar: 15 Draft Taps

The bar is down a couple of steps from the main floor and is bordered on one side by high booth walls, giving it a rather intimate cozy feel. There is a pool table on the upper dining level, along with booths and bench seating towards the back. The bar has an excellent selection of single malts to go along with its definite Scottish flavour. An annual Burns' Night is always booked in advance and so popular that some years they have had to run two. The bar is known to be frequented by the occasional famous face, including Kiefer Sutherland when he's in town. Many traditional dishes are included in the varied menu with the following evening specials: Monday, Wednesday and Saturday: Wings; Tuesday — Fajitas; Thursday — All-you-can-eat pasta; and Friday is the fish and chip dinner. There is a guaranteed lunch menu where it's fifteen minutes or free and appetizers are half price Monday to Friday between 4 PM and 6 PM. The club sandwich comes in the Celtic or the Rangers, your choice. Live bands every Friday night.

Toad in the Hole

Address: 525 King Street West, Toronto
Telephone: 416-593-TOAD
Proprietor: Chris Reid
Opened: 1987
Bar: 11 Draft Taps

A cozy English-style pub located just west of Spadina in the city's popular fashion district. One wall has a series of clocks displaying different time zones, including three which are labeled with local areas — landlord Chris has a dry sense of humour. The pub does boast an interesting collection of prints, many of which are old railway themes. A small but good selection of single malts is available from the bar. The menu features a good cross-section, with many daily specials. Wednesday night and all day Saturday the excellent wings are on special. Live music every Thursday evening.

The Unicorn

Address: 175 Eglinton Avenue East, Toronto
Telephone: 416-482-0115/**Web:** http://www.theunicornpub.com
Proprietor: Elizabeth Luca
Opened: 1980
Bar: 19 Draft Taps

Originally owned by the Irish Rovers and named after one of their biggest hits, this pub was well known for having the longest line-up in the city on St. Patrick's Day. A Tudor-style interior with different levels and numerous nooks and crannies. A large fireplace graces the front dining area. The menu is traditional pub fare with the following evening specials: Monday — Pitcher and wings; Tuesday — Half-price wings; Wednesday — Fiesta night; Friday — Fish and chips; and Saturday: Prime rib. Wednesday is also ladies night with special drinks available for the girls. Live entertainment six nights a week.

The Wheat Sheaf

Corner of King and Bathurst, Toronto
Telephone: 416-504-9912
Manager: Maria
Opened: 1850
Bar: 16 Draft Taps

At the southwest corner of King and Bathurst stands a piece of
Toronto history, the Wheat Sheaf Tavern. Before Canada became a
country, or the automobile was invented, or roads were paved, or
micro breweries became trendy, a young Irish baker named
Bernard Short built this tavern on an obscure crossways outside
the city of Toronto. The bar has survived ever since and is now
protected as a heritage building. Legend has it that a tunnel runs
below connecting it to the old Fort York barracks where soldiers
would sneak away for a quiet pint. Women were finally allowed in
the Wheat Sheaf in 1969. The Sheaf remains today a big part of
the neighbourhood and will probably be here for another hundred
and fifty years. The menu is mostly North American fare and is
available for take-out. There are many daily specials and wings are
half price Sundays, Mondays and Tuesdays after 5 PM.

❖

The Wee Jaggy Nettle

Address: 466 Cosburne Avenue, East York
Telephone: 416-421-4900
Proprietor: Donald MacMillan
Opened: 1996
Bar: 5 Draft Taps

In the running for smallest pub in Ontario, this Scottish pub fits more patrons on its patio than it does inside, where it is licensed for only 25 people. An oak bar with oak flooring around the bar area with the rest of the wee pub carpeted. There are two dartboards available and Scottish posters adorn the walls, including one as you enter with the Scotsman lifting his kilt and inviting you to expose yourself to Scotland. The full menu includes many traditional items. Every second Friday entertainment is in Irish/Celtic mode. The pub may be small but the welcome is big at the Wee Jaggy Nettle.

Wolf and Firkin

Address: 43 Elm Street, Toronto
Telephone: 416-971-6264
Proprietor: Billy Lehman
Opened: 2000
Bar: 16 Draft Taps

A warm and friendly pub on Elm Street just west of Yonge and two streets north of Dundas. As you enter the Wolf from the east, the sit-down bar is down to the south end of this charming and cozy pub. The bar area contains a mixture of high-top tables and two booths. The lower level is the Wolf's Den and this splendid room is available at no charge for private parties. A small patio with seating for 25 sits out front on Elm Street. A full menu with many wonderful daily specials. The wings are on special all day Saturday and Sunday and from 3 until 11 PM throughout the week. Entertainment features live music in the Wolf's Den every Thursday, Friday and Saturday.

The Man of Yorke

Address: 11 Mill Street East, Tottenham
Telephone: 905-936-4486
Proprietor: Mark Whitrod
Opened: 1999
Bar: 12 Draft Taps

This friendly little pub is set in a century building which was originally a blacksmith's shop in the centre of the small but growing community of Tottenham. Landlord Mark hails from Leeds and is an avid Leeds United fan. Many of the soccer scarves hanging around the bar are donated by locals and tourists alike. If a game of darts is not your preference then ask at the bar for the dominoes. The menu is traditional pub fare with daily specials. Entertainment is periodical so please call for details. Tottenham is home to the South Simcoe steam train which runs along the scenic Beeton Valley route; what better way to end your excursion than having a pint and a bite to eat at the Man of Yorke.

The Unionville Arms

Address: 189 Main Street, Unionville
Telephone: 905-470-8831
Proprietors: Paul and Tom
Opened: 1989
Bar: 16 Draft Taps

Located on historical Main Street, which would be a fitting back-drop to many Norman Rockwell prints, this true village pub is the perfect neighbourhood meeting place. The small sit-down bar at the far end of the pub is flanked at the back by the upper dining section partition, making it rather cozy and intimate. The patio at the side of the pub is heated for the days in autumn when the weather is starting to turn. A real sense of community in the bar is shown in the Unionville Arms golf tournament raising almost a quarter of a million dollars for various charities over the years. The menu features traditional and North American dishes, with chef Brian Forbes well known for his culinary specials. Entertainment is every Tuesday and Saturday nights.

Fox and Fiddle

Address: 63 Brock Street West, Uxbridge
Telephone: 905-852-1991
General Manager: Shaun Israelstam
Opened: 1999
Bar: 13 Draft Taps

The main-level sit-down bar is at the front as you enter with the rest of the pub to your right. The whole bar has strategically placed televisions so that never an inning is missed. Downstairs you will find pool tables and weekend entertainment featuring karaoke on Thursday, while Friday and Saturday a disc jockey plays the best dance and retro. The Fox and Fiddle won the Durham region's eat smart award, which recognizes healthy eating and food safety. The menu is very extensive and includes traditional and also a children's menu. A different but delicious dish is the soccer ball sirloin. The pub also carries a good selection of Ontario wines.

The George
Address: 104 Brock Street West, Uxbridge
Telephone: 905-852-9549
Proprietors: John and Maureen
Opened: 1997
Bar: 12 Draft Taps

A large dining section to the left of the bar has all the charm and character of a country home complete with fireplace and antiques. The bar area has a large mirror with the name of the George on it taking up most of one wall. The Uxbridge Tribune readers voted the George as having the best patio and also the best chicken wings in town. The menu is very traditional with a definite English flair which stands to reason as landlord John hails from Liverpool. The full English breakfast proves to be very popular indeed and is served Saturday and Sunday mornings between 9 AM and 12:30 PM. Sunday is also the day of the roast beef dinner special, traditionally done with all the trimmings. Entertainment most weekends, please call for details.

Hobby Horse Arms
Address: 370 Main Street North, Uxbridge
Telephone: 905-852-6126
Proprietor: Nancy Byers
Opened: 1985
Bar: 17 Draft Taps

This century building was lifted from its foundation in 1981 and wheeled through the town of Uxbridge to its present location. Built in the 1860s as a hotel, the pub now offers a quaint downstairs bar complete with an old country fireplace hearth, while upstairs houses a formal dining room. The downstairs bar has an excellent selection of over 140 single malts and a menu with many daily specials and traditional pub fare. The upstairs dining room has an additional capacity of 50 with a separate non-smoking area. The pub holds frequent Scotch nosings, please call for details and dates. The patio overlooks a beautiful garden, which is an annual winner in the Uxbridge in Bloom competition.

Windy O'Neills

Address: 50 Interchange Way, Vaughan
Telephone: 905-760-9366
General Manager: Allan Wilson
Opened: 2000
Bar: 20 Draft Taps

Named after Windy O'Neill who won the Stanley Cup with the
Maple Leafs in 1945, this bar has many different areas to suit any
size of group, from small intimate snugs to a whole bar on the
upper level. The craftsmanship and design of this beautiful pub
have to be seen to be believed: the gantries behind the bar are a
magnificent blend of wood and mirrors and the whole place has
the look of a grand turn-of-the century Dublin hotel. The long
sit-down bar is sectioned by stained glass partitions, while there
are many stone-clad fireplaces throughout the bar, including one
in the Abbey Theatre dining room, with its plush theatre theme. A
large patio sits on the pedestrian thoroughfare of this mini village
with its many restaurants and large movie theatre. The menu is
large and varied, with an excellent selection of Irish traditional
fare. Entertainment Thursday through Saturday, with jazz on the
occasional Sunday.

Studs Lonigans

Address: 168 Main Street, Wasaga Beach
Telephone: 705-429-6371
General Manager: Chris Muirhead
Opened: 1991
Bar: 14 Draft Taps

The large, square sit-down bar is in the middle of this Wasaga pub and it is here you can befriend tourists and locals alike. The pub has a pool table and a shuffleboard at the rear and dartboards are off to the side. A large brick fireplace has a large collection of Toby jugs and steins on its mantle. The pub is adorned throughout with bric a brac including old skis, a turtle shell, bar towels and plenty of soccer scarves. Studs shows all the big games on its giant screen. A large table at the back with long wooden bench seating is perfect for the larger group. A traditional pub menu with the best fish and chips in town. Wednesday is the chicken wings special while Friday features the famous fish and chips. Live entertainment every Wednesday, Friday and Saturday evenings. A very busy spot with tourists in summer and snowmobilers in winter.

❖

The Royal Coachman

Address: 1 Main Street North, Waterdown
Telephone: 905-689-5952
Proprietors: Alex and Marney
Opened: 1995
Bar: 16 Draft Taps

The small town of Waterdown is where you will find this charming red brick pub, built over one hundred years ago. A semi-circular sit-down bar is at the corner of the room while the rest of the area has many comfortable booths throughout. A big-screen TV for all the big games and an area for darts can also be found in the bar, while outside the patio is set apart from the main road by an ivy fence which acts as a buffer against traffic noise and gives a garden touch. Traditional pub fare and more on the menu, with Monday night hosting a very popular fish and chip special. A delicious prime rib dinner is offered on Friday, Saturday and Sunday. Entertainment is periodical so please call for details.

❖

The Duke of Wellington
Address: 33 Erb Street West, Waterloo, 519-886-9370
Proprietor: Frank Riley
Opened: 1980
Bar: 11 Draft Taps

This English-style pub has a large collection of beer bottles and cans from all over the world lining every wall. A large solarium is a great addition to this well-known Waterloo bar and proves to be the most popular lunchtime dining area in the Duke. Every Monday for 14 weeks during the summer the bar hosts an international beer night. Whatever beer is chosen that night, a food special from the same country of origin is available. Menu is mainly traditional fare with an excellent selection of steaks. Glasgow mince and tatties are also listed for the homesick Scot. Entertainment every Thursday, Friday and Saturday evening. A solo blues artist plays on the international beer and food night.

Failte Irish Pub
Address: 85 King Street North, Waterloo
Telephone: 519-747-4530
Proprietors: Brian Watson and Ted Connelly
Opened: 1998
Bar: 13 Draft Taps

A small rustic cottage on the main street of Waterloo houses this friendly neighbourhood Irish pub. Original one-hundred-year-old beams still span the low ceiling, while in areas the original brickwork can still be seen. Stone walls and wooden floors add to the charm and authentic feel of an old Irish country pub. A small courtyard patio can be found at the rear of the building. Traditional pub fare and more, with the wings on special Wednesday nights. Every Monday night has an open jam session, while live entertainment is featured from Thursday night through to Sunday night.

Molly Bloom's

Address: 170 University Avenue, Waterloo
Telephone: 519-885-0892
Proprietor: Desi Fatkin
Opened: 2001
Bar: 11 Draft Taps

Molly's Waterloo opened February 27, 2001, with a seating capacity of 88 and an outside patio with 32. They feature 11 different draft taps, including Moosehead, Keiths and the world famous Guinness. Live entertainment on Thursdays, Fridays and Saturdays, and live entertaining staff the rest of the time! Tuesdays are wing nights, Thursdays are shooter nights, Wednesdays are promotional giveaway nights, and the full menu featuring the famous Guinness-battered fish and chips is available all of the time. They also offer daily features and delicious homemade soups prepared lovingly by their own soup nazi, Rose Mastrangelo. The kitchen is also equipped to honour any menu request due to allergies or health concerns. A big-screen TV is always set to show soccer unless otherwise requested, and the pub opens early for any games during the World Cup season. Molly Bloom's Waterloo is a franchise; the franchisee is Desi Fatkin, be sure to say hello.

Whitby

The Hunter's Horn

Address: 965 Dundas Street West, Unit 14, Whitby
Telephone: 905-665-7395
Proprietor: Peter Swift
Opened: 2000
Bar: 18 Draft Taps

An open-concept pub with a dining area to the right and non-smoking area to the left with the central bar at the far end. Plenty of parking, as the pub is located in a plaza. Only opened a short while, the Hunter's Horn has already established itself in the area and has built up a steady clientele. A small patio is out front along with the red British phone box. Traditional fare and more on the varied menu with many daily specials. Monday is wing night, Tuesday is pasta night and Wednesday is the popular fish and chip night. Entertainment features the best of local musicians every Saturday night.

❖

Leepers Landing

Address: 227 Brock Street South, Whitby
Telephone: 905-666-2211
Proprietors: Peter Nelipa, Rich White and Sean Kunkel
Opened: 1998
Bar: 16 Draft Taps

Leepers Landing gives you the best of both worlds, with a pub on the main level with two fireplaces, cozy booths and wing-back chairs, while upstairs is a popular dance bar featuring a disc jockey every Thursday, Friday and Saturday night. The menu is a North American mix with many daily specials, including wings on Tuesdays and Thursdays. The main floor bar has retro rock and roll every Thursday evening with Mike Hall, Darren Smith and guests. Live bands also on Friday and Saturdays.

The Pub at Pearson Lanes

Address: 101 Mary Street, Whitby
Telephone: 905-430-5699
General Manager: John Blackburn
Opened: 2000
Bar: 16 Draft Taps

The beautiful old Sebert House was once a livery stable in 1914 and in the past has been moved from its foundations three times before reaching its present address where it has remained for the last 10 years. With plenty of charm and comfortable sections, the bar has a warm and inviting feeling. The menu is extensive and features mainly Canadian fare, with lunch and dinner specials. Monday is mussel night, Tuesday is two-for-one wing night and Thursday is a pasta special. Karaoke on Thursday, and live bands on Friday and Saturday.

The Tap and Tankard

Address: 224 Brock Street South, Whitby
Telephone: 905-666-8090
Proprietors: James Jaap and David Brouse
Opened: 1997
Bar: 21 Draft Taps

The large patio at the rear of this pub, complete with its own bar, is heated and can be covered to keep it open all year round. A busy weekend spot, this pub has a long sit-down bar and a well-needed stand-up bar. There is a small fireside lounge off to one side with comfortable seating and a pool table at the end of the bar. A great selection of draft beers and an equally good selection of single malts. The menu is a very large selection of traditional pub fare and lots more, including excellent salads and sandwiches. Tuesday is two-for-one pizza night, Wednesday is wing night, and Sunday has a prime rib dinner special as well as two-for-one fajitas. The Tap shows all major soccer games. Entertainment nightly from Thursday through to Sunday, please call for details.

Patrick O'Ryan's

Address: 25 Pitt Street East, Windsor
Telephone: 519-977-5722
Proprietor: Chris Ryan
Opened: 1996
Bar: 25 Draft Taps

Just around the corner from the Windsor casino, this traditional Irish pub caters to many American visitors from the Detroit area. The walls have many Irish murals and prints throughout. A large Harp mirror sits over a stone-clad fireplace in the dining area. Along with the many beers on tap, the pub also has a good selection of single malts and Irish whiskies. A banquet hall upstairs can be booked for functions and the bar will cater to any special culinary needs. A large menu with a hearty Irish fare section. Friday and Saturday has live bands upstairs and solo or duo acts downstairs. So if you are planning a trip to the casino make sure you pop in for a visit to this friendly Irish pub.

Woodbridge

Moose and Firkin

Address: 7600 Weston Road, Units 13 and 15, Woodbridge
Proprietor: Sherry Hulburd
Opened: 2000
Bar: 16 Draft Taps

The Moose is Woodbridge's local English-style pub and is fast becoming a favourite spot in this expanding community. Situated in a plaza, the pub has plenty of parking and a small outside patio. The bar is a mixture of booths and tables and there is a pool table to the side. A private room is available for functions. A traditional and North American menu with great daily specials. Wing nights are every Sunday, Monday and Saturday. The Moose has entertainment Sunday afternoons and Tuesday and Friday evenings. The pub is open to 2 AM seven nights a week.

Woodstock

Charles Dickens

Address: 505 Dundas Street, Woodstock
Telephone: 519-421-2218
Proprietor: Joan Hodder
Opened: 1996
Bar: 16 Draft Taps

A very traditional English-style pub with plenty of authentic English prints and memorabilia throughout. The pub is fast becoming the place to eat in town as word spreads about the exceptional quality of the menu, and dinner time testifies to this with the dining area being very busy. The Dickens is also a very friendly pub where the regulars make you feel right at home. The pub shows all major soccer games and there is a "friendly" rivalry among the many English and Scottish patrons. The menu is mainly traditional pub fare, with the fish and chips the most popular by far. Wednesday is wing and sing night featuring wing specials and karaoke. Entertainment at the weekends twice monthly, please call for details.

❖

Index of Pubs

Index of Pubs

❖